"How to Succeed at Planning and Goal Setting Workbook"

Individual Strategic Planning

James S. Gordon

Table of Contents

Page 6   **Dedication**

Page 7   **Acknowledgments**

Page 8   **Preface**

Page 10   **Introduction**

Page 11   **CHAPTER 1 - Why Should I Have an Individual Strategic Plan?**
Page 11   **Does Your Organization Have A Strategic Plan?**
Page 12   **Why Have An Individual Strategic Plan?**
Page 12   **What Is An Individual Strategic Plan?**
Page 12   **Who Uses An Individual Strategic Plan?**
Page 13   **When Do I Begin Using Individual Strategic Planning?**
Page 13   **The Value Syllogism**

Page 15   **CHAPTER 2 - Activity Management System**
Page 15   **Getting Started**
Page 16   **Retrospective on Time Management**
Page 17   **Time Logs**
Page 18   **How Long Should I Keep Track Of My Time?**
Page 18   **Time Wasters**
Page 19   **Failure of Time Management Systems**
Page 20   **Chart of Accounts**
Page 20   **Chart of Time Accounts**
Page 22   **Nesting of Time Concepts**
Page 24   **Time Management Epitaph**
Page 24   **Morphing an Icon**
Page 24   **Prospecting For Goal(s)**
Page 26   **What's Next?**

Page 28   **Chapter 3 - Goal Mining Part 1 - Goal Discovery**
Page 28   **Other Goal Setting Systems**

Page 28   **Assumptions about Goals**
Page 29   **One Wish**
Page 31   **Tried And True Goal Setting Systems**
Page 33   **Pseudo-Goals**
Page 34   **Unspoken Goals**
Page 34   **What Becomes A Goal?**
Page 35   *****Goals Mini-Glossary**
Page 37   **Goal Discovery and Distillation**
Page 38   **SELF-IMAGE**
Page 40   **School-Image Grid**
Page 41   **TEAM-IMAGE**
Page 43   **Goal Tree:**
Page 43   **Goal Tree Exercise**
Page 55   **The Fruit of the Goal Tree**

Page 56   **Chapter 4, Goal Mining - Part 2, The Goal Distillation Process**
Page 57   **The Goal Grid**
Page 61   **Goal Conflicts**
Page 62   **Goal Circles**
Page 64   **Daily Tasks**
Page 64   **Linked To Do List**

Page 69   **Chapter 5 – A Model for success**
Page 69   **Success – Definitions**
Page 70   **Cognitive Dissonance**
Page 71   **Success Models – Individual Models**
Page 72   **Success Models – Team/Group Models**
Page 73   **"DEJA VU" Success Revisited**
Page 76   **The Expertise Matrix**
Page 77   **Expertise Matrix Example**
Page 77   **Designing an Expertise Matrix**

Page 79   **Chapter 6 - Building and Maintaining a Success Inventory**
Page 79   **The Success Inventory**
Page 79   **Assessing Our Resources and Barriers to Success**

Page 83   Personal Employment Planning Profile
Page 84   Networking
Page 85   Networking Form

Page 87   **Chapter 7 - Metrics**
Page 87   **METRICS**
Page 88   **Clues – Success**
Page 89   **Clues – Failure**
Page 90   **POINT SCHEDULE**
Page 92   **THE PROSPERITY CALENDAR**
Page 94   **Next Use of Funds Statement**
Page 95   **Entry Strategies**
Page 96   **Exit Strategies**
Page 97   **Debriefing Strategy**

Page 98   **Chapter 8 - The Wrap-up**
Page 98   **"Final Product" Checklist**
Page 99   **The Follow-up Schedule**
Page 101   **MOTIVATION**

Page 102   **Chapter 9 - Special Preview**
Page 102   **Idea Realization Continuum**
Page 103   **Strategic Alignment of Your Job Description w/Your Organization's Vision and Mission**
Page 104   **Risk Management**
Page 104   **Failure Management**
Page 105   **Employee Footprint**

Page 106   **ASSESSMENT (Back-end)**

Page 110   **Postscript**

Page 111   **APPENDIX A**

Page 116   **APPENDIX B**

How to *Succeed* at Personal Planning and Goal Setting Workbook (Individual Strategic Planning)

by

James S. Gordon

DEDICATION

Who do I include in my dedication? Who do I exclude? With my first book, I will dedicate it to the people who made my education feel like the most important endeavor in my life.

That list starts with the aunt and uncle who raised me, Mrs. Mabel Penrice Inman and her husband, Augustus E. Inman. My brother, Robert J. Keyes and my sister, Mabel Keyes Ackerson both made a point of staying in touch with me and encouraging me to graduate when I went away to college. The rest of my family was supportive, but the aforementioned family members went the extra mile(s).

I'd be remiss not to mention my brother, Will, because I am not quite sure if he kept me pushing harder or if I kept him pushing harder – towards graduation(s). The truth is that we probably kept each other headed toward our respective goals. And, Uncle Leon Gordon is still "cheer-leading" the completion of my Ph.D. – thanks – I'll get there.

My dedication extends to a few teachers at Columbus Elementary in Berkeley, CA who really made a difference. Mrs. Comoford rewarded me with a $3 prize for winning a spelling bee in 3rd grade; Mr. DeSoto (5th grade) helped me to believe that I could do anything - academically, and Mr. Ong (6th grade) helped me to understand the role of discipline and integrity in education. Each of these teachers made it their business to encourage me.

Without a doubt, Mrs. Curtiss at Berkeley High School was the most helpful in terms of encouraging and assisting me with my writing skills. Mrs. Curtiss published one of my short stories and suggested that I continue to write. Another high school teacher, Mr. William Reidsma, was a close second in terms of encouraging me to write more. Mr. Reidsma published one of my Haiku poems (I have since written over 100 Haiku poems).

I, now, know why so many writers thank their significant others in their dedications. In part, that significant other sacrifices her or his time and energy right along with the writer. Thank you, Bonnie, I will make it all worthwhile.

ACKNOWLEDGMENTS

This acknowledgement is intended to express my gratitude to the mentors in my life. Some of those "mentors" were authors who inspired that which is creative in me, that which is imaginative in me, that which is compassionate in me, that which is analytical in me, and that which is genuine in me.

The most influential mentors were the supervisors I worked for in my first job - after college. That job was at Caltech's Jet Propulsion Laboratory (JPL) in Pasadena, CA. These mentors poured a lot of themselves into me - in the hopes that some of it would rub off - it finally did.

The characteristics that I admire most in people these mentors embodied. I could not have asked for a better start to my professional life than what I experienced at JPL.

My heartfelt gratitude goes to (my direct supervisors) Robert J. Hansen, Thomas R. Stewart, Robert M. Cass, Gordon O. Boles, John Bogard, and Stanley Locke. Additionally, I am, also, grateful to co-workers, Jack Adams, Lowell Anderson, Janet Musial, Leon Mosby, Jr., S. Hector Arambulo, and Lee City. I consider myself fortunate that I have been able to maintain contact with both Leon and Hector – thanks for being my friends.

Preface

In a more perfect world, you might expect to read a single self-help book, become motivated, and subsequently overcome your barriers to success - living happily ever after. However, I did not experience that more perfect world as the single book idea did not work for me. And, maybe it is not working or did not work for you, either.

This workbook is a product of thirty years of my experience reading hundreds of books and articles, listening to tapes, attending lectures, attending workshops, and working as an assistant and protégé of accomplished people in business. Many of the forms and lists contained in this workbook are "Heuristic" products - developed from my diverse experiences in human resources, workforce development, economic development, financial services, and self-employment.

Some of the forms and the enclosed "musings" are products of my academic pursuits. My three year doctoral degree program will now take me six years to complete (I have yet to complete my dissertation). My twenty-three years of formal education has afforded me the luxury of reading and observing some of the best practices in education and training. And, it is the product of my education and experience that I am offering to you.

Upon completing this workbook, you will be able to:

1. List three activities that you desire most to do along with three activities that you need most to do.
2. Prioritize the desires and needs listed in #1.
3. Set daily to do activities based on your desires and needs.
4. Name (and give examples of) at least four Activity Management Concepts.
5. Name 5 Critical Success Factors and 5 Critical Failure Factors in the individual strategic planning process.
6. List at least three components of the Expertise Matrix.
7. Create a follow-up schedule to keep your plan on track to completion.
8. Name three success traits that you admire in others or seek to attain.
9. List at least three entry strategies and three exit strategies for joining a group, team, organization, or activity.
10. And much more!

I welcome your feedback as we improve the information contained in this workbook.

Leap Frogging

Although, leap frog refers to a game that many children, around the world, learn to play - it has applications to the work that I envision with this workbook. Specifically, I plan to update the workbook - from time to time - by incorporating some of the musings contained, herein. I will, also, incorporate some of the improvements that come from readers and users of this Goal Discovery and Distillation Process, thereby, giving readers the opportunity to "continuously improve" as they customize their individual strategic plans.

Organizational strategic plans may, some day, incorporate the individual strategic plans of individuals who engage in the development of their own strategic plans - benefiting themselves and their organizations.

Musings

My musings are included because I see areas for development even before this volume has been completed. Some of these developments, I can do alone. Other developments are multi - disciplinary in nature, and will require that I consult with experts in the areas of consideration.

If I had tried to incorporate all the musings that I now have for this workbook, I would have a book approaching a thousand pages or more. I don't recall the last time that I picked up a 1,000 page book, can you?

I anticipate that there will be readers who will add to this work in numerous ways. My advice is please leap frog my efforts, here.

How to Use This Work Book?

This book is essentially a workbook whether in electronic or print form. It is only through your inputs that this volume comes to life - generating a dynamic plan and process to help you realize your dreams and aspirations. This process works as you work it - yielding benefits for you and/or those close to you - including those people who look to you for guidance.

Complete each step and you will have a series of snapshots of your life and what you want it to become, i.e. a moving picture of you becoming, obtaining, doing, and sharing the best of you.

Notes on this electronic version

There were scores of edits in an effort to "perfect" this workbook during the last 30 days prior to its submission and publication as a Kindle ebook. The most difficult part of writing the book was the adaptation of the graphics to the Kindle format. I am not yet satisfied with the "final product" in terms of the legibility of the graphics. But, I take consolation in knowing that the graphics problem is solved for the paperback workbook.

As an aid to you, I have attempted to describe the contents of each form so that you can use the form in developing your individual strategic plan. Those of you who have a Kindle app for PC or MAC, or an iPad will find that the graphics are a tad more legible on those devices. I assure you that we will continue to work on this problem in the future.

Introduction

Have you ever participated in an organization's strategic planning process? If so, how much time, money, and staff were committed to developing that strategic plan? Oftentimes, a consultant or facilitator is hired to keep the process on track towards specific targets. Some organizations will rent (or buy) a facility for a retreat - paying the cost of travel and lodging for its staff. Even if your organization did not hire an external consultant, it is likely that the strategic planning process involved top management's time for a period of 2-5 days, at a minimum.

My point is that a high degree of value is placed on obtaining the results of this strategic planning exercise. My questions to you are - does your organizations offer / pay for individuals to develop their own individual strategic plans? Have you had the opportunity to develop an individual strategic plan? Have you ever completed a personal strategic plan of any kind?

One might ask the question, how effective can a strategic planner be for an organization if she has not taken the time and developed the knowledge of what to do and how to do it in terms of personally planning her own life? Is she putting her best foot forward, so to speak? Would she be more effective after such an investment of time and money in her own strategic plan? Maybe!

The information and exercises in this workbook are designed to assist each reader with the tasks of developing answers to the foregoing questions. Whether you are a career counselor, parent, student, educator, entrepreneur, public or private employee, or retiree, you will find ideas and exercises to help you with the detailed thinking and planning activities which will bring you success at goal-setting and life planning.

CHAPTER 1 - Why Should I Have an Individual Strategic Plan?

- Does Your Organization Have A Strategic Plan?
- What Is An Individual Strategic Plan?
- Why Have An Individual Strategic Plan?
- Who Uses An Individual Strategic Plan?
- When Does One Need An Individual Strategic Plan?
- Value Syllogism

Does Your Organization Have A Strategic Plan?

It is likely that I am not unique in terms of sitting in on or being invited to attend a strategic planning activity or retreat and then wondering why so much time and money were being invested in the activity when I have spent relatively little time in planning my own life. There just seems to be so little time after work and/or school and/or family commitments to do anything just for me.

Someday, we think that we will sit down and work on a strategic planning-type exercise for ourselves, which will yield basic information about our strengths, weaknesses, opportunities and threats [SWOT]. Then days, months, and years pass without completing, or in some cases, without starting that strategic or life plan. And with the best of intentions, we are now 30, 40, 50, 60, or 70+ years of age. The promise to do it someday has begun to haunt us. We may even pick up a book or two to help us to begin the process. But, somehow the help that we seek may still elude us.

It has been my experience - over the past 30+ years - instructing thousands of workshop participants - that many times we are told what to do, but not how to do it. For example, if I were a master mechanic and you brought me your car for repairs and I told you that you will need to overhaul your engine yourself, if you wish to save money. I have just told you what to do, but you may have no clue as to how to get the engine out of your car, inspect the parts, machine or replace certain parts, re-assemble, and you may not have the time, tools, or the space to accomplish this goal, either.

We may tell our teenagers to be conscientious or reliable, but that suggestion may not be helpful to them as communicating what the terms "conscientious" or "reliable" mean was not done. Without that missing information, that teen cannot do "conscientious" or do "reliable" until its meaning has been **broken down** and communicated to her. Part of the breaking down of the message is to identify the behaviors that are requisite to the state that we call conscientious or reliable.

Individual Strategic Planning begins and completes this process of obtaining the "what" and "how" of developing a workable and flexible individualized strategic planning model. We begin by asking (and answering) the following questions.

Why Have An Individual Strategic Plan?

Because, we are worth the effort, time, and money needed to complete our own individual strategic plans. Are you currently in a career that resonates with your aspirations and/ or dreams? Are you in a career that meets your needs for belonging and recognition? Does your organization invest in you as an individual? Are the employees or stakeholders in your organization committed to the vision and mission of your organization - because your organization's vision and mission are congruent with your (and their) own life's vision and mission? If the answer(s) is no, the work that we do below will help.

Is your significant other's or child(ren)'s goal(s) congruent with your own goals? If not, the work that we do, below, will help you. And, if your answer was yes to the questions in this section, you will be prepared for the time when there are changes in the directions and goals between you and those close to you or with your employer.

What Is An Individual Strategic Plan?

An Individual Strategic Plan entails detailed personal planning for an individual. This planning yields real desires, needs, and priorities for the individual. Developing an individual strategic plan will lead to the reduction of or elimination of goal conflicts, your resources will be identified, and your barriers will be identified and overcome.

Who Uses An Individual Strategic Plan?

An individual who wants to find her heart's desire, reduce her career indecision, help her children (or mate) make sound personal and life decisions, or who wants to be the best possible contributor to her organization's or business' success.

A stay-at-home parent, an entrepreneur, executive, entry-level new hire, and a full-time student are prime candidates for an individual strategic plan. An individual strategic plan is critical for anyone in transition from school-to-work, work-to-school, work-to-retirement, or contemplating a new job or career. Even a single person planning to marry is a good candidate for Individual Strategic Planning.

One of the underlying principles of this workbook is that you are the world's foremost expert and authority on what you dream about, love to do, like to do, should do, have to do, or do not like to do, etc. With the tools in this workbook, you will discover what your wants and needs are. This process will then help you to prioritize and balance your efforts towards attaining both your needs and your wants. In addition, you will be able to coordinate your wants and needs with the significant other people in your life. Everyone close to you can now benefit from your newly acquired expertise!

When Do I Begin Using Individual Strategic Planning?

Inputs to the individual strategic planning process (e.g. the Goal Tree and Goal Grid) may begin to be developed in middle school, high school or college. These inputs can be aggregated into a life plan and updated on a regular basis. An individual strategic plan can also be very helpful to someone planning to retire within a 3-5 year time horizon or that is in retirement - but contemplating or experiencing a life changing event.

The Value Syllogism

So far, we have established that organizations place value, i.e. they spend time and money on the development of strategic plans. These organizations are for-profit corporations as well as governmental agencies and non-profits.

All the organizations that I have worked for and worked with have had a policy or philosophy (statement) of valuing their people or human resources.

If organizations value strategic planning (for the organization) as indicated by the time and money dedicated to these processes; and, if those organizations also value their human resources, doesn't it stand to reason that those organizations would also value strategic planning for their human resources?

organizational strategic planning=valuable
organizations=people
people=individual(s)

people=valuable
strategic planning for individuals=valuable

To say or reason otherwise would upset the widely-held value proposition that we display in many of our organizations - telling all that we recognize that people are our most valuable resource.

Even if the foregoing syllogism were not true, I believe that many or most people value themselves and when given a set of tools to improve themselves - most will do so - with or without permission from the organizations that employ them.

However, quality organizations will recognize this upward movement of their people and those organizations will find a way to accommodate or **collaborate** with employees who choose to create individual strategic plans.

You Are the World's Foremost Expert And Authority on

Your Dreams, Loves, Desires, and Likes

As well as Your Shoulds, Musts, Have Tos, and Dislikes

Musing RE: *Employer Accommodation Quotient* as it pertains to the incorporation and use of Individual Strategic Planning by employees / stakeholders of organizations.

I look forward to a time when we have conducted substantial research on the use of individual strategic planning for employees of an organization to determine if there is a benefit to doing so versus continuing with the status quo of "trickle-down" strategic planning.

At present, I assume people will use individual strategic planning whether or not the practice is encouraged, condoned, or frowned upon in one's organization. I know that you will be both enlightened and enriched by engaging in individual strategic planning. The learning organization a la Peter Senge will find a way to accommodate the enlightenment and enrichment to you - that our system promises.

Individual strategic planning and traditional organizational strategic planning must not just co-exist, these processes must become interdependent or better yet - interoperable.

CHAPTER 2 - Activity Management System

- Getting Started
- Retrospective on Time Management
- Time Logs
- How Long Should I Keep Track of My Time?
- Time Wasters
- Failure of Time Management Systems
- Chart of Time Accounts
- Nesting of Time Concepts
- Time Management Epitaph
- Prospecting for Goal(s)

Getting Started

Have you ever heard a boss tell her employee or a parent tell her child to straighten up or be more conscientious or more dependable? One might argue that the employee or child is insubordinate if she does not follow orders. But, without feedback, how do we know that the employee or child knows how to do what she was ordered to do? What behaviors must the employee (or child) exhibit in order to comply with her boss' order? Can you do "conscientious" or do "dependable"? What does each word mean? How will she know that she has achieved her goal of becoming conscientious or dependable?

The answers to these questions will be examined in more detail in Chapter 3. But for now, suffice it to say certain goals or results cannot be attained without additional information or elucidation. Remember, telling someone to do something is not the same as (also) telling or showing them how to do it.

In this workbook, I will show you how to discover what is most important to you and illustrate a means to accomplish that which you envision to do, to obtain, or to attain.

A former supervisor once told me a story of a handyman who was called in to fix a woman's furnace. He brought his toolbox in with him and went down to the basement where the furnace was. He piddled about for a few minutes, then took out his mallet - gave the furnace a couple of firm taps - and behold it started right up as good as new. He wrote up his invoice, he then took it upstairs to the homeowner who remarked $100.00 - how come it costs so much - you were down there for only a few minutes? He retorted, I charged you $5 for my time and $95 for knowing where to focus my attention. You, too, will be able to know where and how to direct you life's energy in terms of discovering, planning, and executing that plan.

I have run into many people who don't believe that they have the time to make the required changes in their lives. And for those who do have the time, some do not feel that they have the tools to make the change happen. Thus, the first step in the direction of change is assessing our time concepts and the current use of our 24-hour day(s).

Retrospective on Time Management

A few years after graduating from college, I met Dr. Rob Rutherford who was consulting with Caltech in Pasadena, CA. Dr. Rutherford conducted Time Management workshops for the employees of Caltech's Jet Propulsion Laboratory at the Industrial Relations Center in Pasadena. Employees of the Lab lauded the benefits of incorporating time management techniques into their hectic and demanding schedules at work and at home.

Contemporaneously with Dr. Rutherford's workshops, were workshops presented by staff of the late Bill Oncken. Mr. Oncken was renowned for his "Managing Management Time" or the Getting the Monkey Off Your Back workshops. These were very entertaining as well as useful aids to supervisors and managers at the Lab.

The third time management workshop that I had the pleasure to be involved in was a Time Management workshop created by that aforementioned supervisor, RJM. RJM created his workshop using information and tools gleaned from Alan Lakein, author of "How to Get Control of Your Time and Your Life" and Alec MacKenzie, author of "The Time Trap".

Along with all of the foregoing training, I have read other books and numerous articles on Time Management. One of the ironies that I have observed over the past three decades is that Americans have become more time-pressured rather than less so - despite the variety of resources available to us.

It is a trite phrase, but we cannot manage time - we can only manage ourselves. Nonetheless, most time management programs leave us at the mercy of onerous time-wasters, which subvert our best intentions of having a productive day(s). That feeling can be a thing of the past as we re-orient our thinking towards an Activity Management System - relieving ourselves of the burden of carrying time on our collective shoulders.

Time Logs

Before we consign Time Management to the proverbial scrapheap of history, let's preserve its best elements as there is no need to re-invent the wheel when useful tools exist. The most useful tool of the time management systems that I have learned is the Time Log. A Time Log is a tool, which provides us with the opportunity to record the various activities that we engage in each day. Some people will record activities on a 15-min basis, others on a 30-min basis, and still others on a 60-min basis. As a rule of thumb, the busier your day is in terms of the number of things that you typically do - the more likely you will need a Time Log which uses 15 minute intervals. Here is an example of a time log:

Time Log

Time:	Monday	Tuesday	Wednesday	Thursday	Friday	Saturday	Sunday
			Time Logs				
8am							
8:15am							
8:30am							
8:45am							
9am							
9:15am							
9:30am							
9:45am							
10am							
10:15am							
10:30am							
10:45am							
11am							
11:15am							
11:30am							
11:45am							
Noon							
12:15pm							
12:30pm							
12:45pm							
1pm							
1:15pm							
1:30pm							
1:45pm							
2pm							
2:15pm							
2:30pm							
2:45pm							
3pm							
3:15pm							
3:30pm							
3:45pm							
4pm							
4:15pm							
4:30pm							
4:45pm							
5pm							

By the way, the Time Journal is another method of recording time that I found useful. A Time Journal has no delineations as to minutes spent on a given task. What one does is to record her or his activities on a legal pad or blank sheet of paper in the sequence that the activities occur. One even has the liberty to write a retrospective on each day's activities - at the end of the day. An alternative to this approach is to use a digital recorder to catalog the day's activities and the time that each occurs throughout one's day. This is also considered a Time Journal.

Variations of the Monday-Friday 15 minute interval format, include:

1. A six or seven day format - your choice as some individuals work week-ends and nights.
2. A twenty-four hour day rather than an eighteen hour day - a twelve-hour day is also acceptable.
3. Some individuals like an open format, i.e. Morning, Afternoon, and Evening or Night rather than a minute-by-minute or hour-by-hour Time Log.

How Long Should I Keep Track Of My Time?

I am not aware of any research on an optimal amount of time to keep track of one's time. However, the more days that you engage in this activity the more diverse (or alike in some cases) your days may become. If possible or practical for you, include weekends and evenings, if you work a daily schedule. And, if you work nights or week-ends, please record your daytime and week day activities as you are able.

Time Wasters

The most energetic discussions during Time Management workshops that I conducted were the discussions of Time Wasters, usually, in break-out groups. When our groups reconvened, we recorded input from each group. The range of recorded activities could run from taking drop-in visitors who just wanted to chat to standing meetings wherein the participant was the recipient of updates and emergency edicts from top management - and everything in between. But, as I recall, the most common time waster was something we refer to as procrastination. Many tales of woe ensued as we listened to participant after participant detail how she or he got into trouble as a result of putting something off.

The other part of the exercise - after the venting - was an attempt to discuss ways to overcome or cope with the time waster - to become more productive. After years of teaching some variation of the theme of becoming more disciplined - concerning procrastination, I received a "bombshell" of an announcement while listening to a National Public Radio (NPR) broadcast one morning. A report on the research of Dr. Neil Fiore, a UC-Berkeley scientist revealed that, and I paraphrase, procrastination is not a problem - it is a way of coping with problems. That is, when we are faced with a problem, we decide to put off resolving the problem as a coping mechanism, which provides us a modicum of relief for the moment. And, inevitably, there will be some things that go away due to a lack of attention. But, in my experience, that is the exception.

Our discussion of time management now changes its focus towards activity management - something that is within our control - rather than a continued focus on the hands of a clock. I encourage you to continue using Time Logs to evaluate or audit your current time usage. However, our new approach quickly diverges from the classical time management training. Before we explain what a chart of accounts entails, let's look at some reasons why time management strategies might fail.

Failure of Time Management Systems

In retrospect, some of the time management programs that I participated in focused - too heavily - on a single tool or technique. For example, a focus would be on the time logs and the periodic use of these tools to re-visit the activities that consumed our time. Or, reserving the first 15-60 minutes a day for repose or planning. These types of tools or techniques - alone may diminish in value - if used in isolation.

Another shortcoming of classical time management training was the "mythologies" of time management. The prime myth is that time can be managed - it cannot. Above, procrastination was revealed to be more than putting things off until another time, yet the myth of procrastination continues to be discussed in time management literature as a time waster.

The phrase in the footer of the "Expertise Matrix graphic (Chapter 5) states, "The genesis of wasted time is in time spent on unwritten goals". The importance of this statement is in the implication that one may not know or judge an activity as a waste of time unless there is a metric against which it can be measured.

The Activity Management System consists of a new set of constructs for the interpretation of time usage that does not make one a slave of a ticking clock. Thus, relieving us of a burden of counting minutes and hours rather than living those minutes and hours - more fully. Our Activity Management System is anchored to a planning system [in subsequent chapters], which allows one to explore the depth and breadth of her desires and needs to be, do, obtain, and share more.

Chart of Accounts

In general, anyone who manages a household or a business (or business unit) has a chart of accounts. On this chart of accounts are the expenses or costs of running that household or business, e.g. rent, mortgage or lease payments; utilities; insurance; food; entertainment; travel; transportation; etc. Some of these costs are fixed or stay the same each month and others are variable or subject to change - from time to time. The income or revenue stream may (or may not) be steady each month. From that income or revenue one may plan the expenses that she can comfortably afford.

Our Activity Management System is "loosely" analogous to this chart of accounts in that each individual has a 24-hour per day "income" or "revenue" stream of time. However, each of us differs in terms of the type of activities that we engage in each day - our individual "chart of time accounts".

From our respective 24-hour days, we engage in work, school, eating, sleeping, playing, talking, driving, planning, watching television or movies, reading, exercise, etc. The chart of time accounts consists of the following components:

1. **Result Time**
2. **Event Time**
3. **Emergency Time**
4. **Found Time**
5. **Amorphous Time**
6. **Unstructured Time**
7. **Transition Time**

Next, we will discuss each of these activity management components in more detail.

Chart of Time Accounts

1. Result Time [Keyword = Participant] --- Our focus is on the desired outcome or end result of an activity - rather than on how long it takes us to achieve the outcome. We focus on participation in an activity versus watching others act. For example:

1. Going to a job interview
2. Going on a first date
3. Picking up your children from school
4. Celebrating your wedding anniversary
5. Going to a doctor's appointment

You are an active participant in the foregoing activities and you have a stake in the positive outcome or results in each case.

2. Event Time [Keyword = Spectator] --- We engage in Event Time, when we spend time in an activity, which usually has a known time commitment as we watch others act, e.g.:

1. Going to a movie or watching a movie
2. Watching a television show
3. Attending a sporting event
4. Attending someone else's wedding as a guest

We assume a passive role in Event Time while others are doing or participating in activities that we choose to watch.

3. Emergency Time [Keyword = Supplant or Displace] --- We experience Emergency Time, when an incident occurs which precludes or displaces our engaging in activities that were [initially] scheduled or planned or are actually being engaged in, e.g.:

1. House fire
2. Death of a family member or close friend
3. Major illness or injury to you or someone you care for
4. Act of God, i.e. earthquake, tornado, hurricane, etc.
5. Irate Customer who walks in to or calls your organization
6. Sudden loss (quit / firing / injury / re-assignment) of a co- worker

We must, typically, stop what we are doing to re-focus our attention on the emergency. Attending the emergency may cause us to transition into another state or type of time.

4. Found Time [Keywords = Freed Up] --- We experience Found Time when our time is freed up due to the cessation of time spent elsewhere, such as with Result Time, Emergency Time, or Amorphous Time. Examples include:

1. Upon completion of a degree program, the graduate will gain 10-20+ hours a week for other activities
2. After the death or recovery of a loved one or friend there is a re-allocation of time for the care-giver
3. Receiving a job offer [starting a job] after a period of unemployment OR losing a job and beginning a job search.

5. Amorphous Time [Keyword = Increments] --- We experience Amorphous Time as activities or a series of activities for which an accurate prediction of time needed for completion cannot be easily ascertained, e.g.:

1. Finding a new job
2. Getting well again
3. Finding a mate
4. Learning a language
5. Potty training a child

We all find it desirable or necessary to engage in Amorphous Time as we cannot attain instant gratification in some of the things that we do. We must persist in engaging in the series of activities which lead us to the outcome or desired result, which is obtained or attained via Amorphous Time pursuits.

6. Unstructured Time [Keyword = Uncommitted] --- Going into a block of time with no commitments, plans, or desires to do or schedule any given activity. We can, pro-actively, reserve blocks of time wherein no commitments are made to attain, obtain, or do a thing. Uncertainty may also be an element of Unstructured Time.

7. Transition Time [Keywords = Changing States] --- Moving from one time or state to the next wherein processing, transitioning, or shifting of gears occurs.

1. Driving home from work may require some degree of decompressing or release of the pressures of work OR going to work may require psyching oneself up for the day.
2. Participating in an athletic or other competitive endeavor may also require engaging in specific preparations or routines.
3. Any or each transition to a new state or Activity Management component could entail a transition phase with an unknown amount of time needed to accomplish the transition.

Nesting of Time Concepts

If you own Tupperware or Rubbermaid storage containers, you have likely seen the type of containers that are stored one inside of another - from the smallest containers to the largest ones. This phenomenon is known as nesting. And, in our Activity Management System, one type of time can be nested in another. For example, in examining the so-called time waster of a phone call, we observe the following.

Sara: Jim, this is Sara in Graphics, we received your PowerPoint presentation, but we will not be able to meet your 72-hour turnaround for completion.

Jim: Sara, I am sorry to hear that. So, what are my options?

Sara: We have had good success with a local firm that will take this type of job, 24/7. Shall I contact them for you?

Jim: Please do. Sara, is there a surcharge or rush fee? If so, how much?

Sara: It is about 20%, but it will come out of our budget not yours.

Jim: Thanks, again. By the way, I saw you and your daughter at the recital last night. Your daughter looks like she is ready for Carnegie Hall.

Sara: Funny you should mention that, she just received a letter from Julliard...

Jim was interrupted from his work by the call from Sara. However, Sara was calling him about an important business matter. Under the Activity Management System, this call would be categorized as a result time activity. However, within this context of result time came the nesting effect of/by transitioning to the recollection of or re-living of the event time spent at the recital the previous evening. The interruption was not a time waster neither was it solely a result-oriented activity nor an event-oriented activity - it was (led to) a nested activity within the meaning of the new *overlay* of Activity Management.

If you found yourself in a waiting room for a doctor's appointment [a result time activity] and your appendix burst you would transition from result time to emergency time wherein a new result was nested, i.e. removing the appendix. Your recovery time is best described as amorphous time as no one can predict how long it will take. But, within the context of recovery or amorphous time, you may be able to achieve given results related to family, work, or school.

There is a chance that the two parties involved in a first date may have different judgments regarding the nature of the time to be spent on a date. One party might see the date as a result in terms of making a new friend (and more). The other party might see 1) a nested event leading to… 2) an amorphous finding a mate activity 3) an emergency.

The nesting of time can take place in meetings, on phone calls, or with drop-in visitors or in a host of other scenarios. Nesting of time takes place in personal matters as well.

I believe it prudent to withhold judgment about time wasting as there is another way to look at our time usage. Furthermore, why feel guilty about or make others feel guilty about their usage of time?

Time Management Epitaph

I am not ready to write such an epitaph on time management systems, because, on the whole, my experiences have been positive. I have even taught others to use the techniques in these systems. I believe that both systems can co-exist. However, the more important question is that of having a nexus to a suitable planning system to link the Activity Management or Time Management system to. The reason for this is [the pursuit of] worthwhile goals and objectives populate the time logs and assessments that people make in auditing or gauging their progress towards their goals.

Morphing an Icon

Some people might ask, what does an Activity Management System have to do with individual strategic planning? Briefly, this new way of looking at our time and the things that we do with our time, can free up the time needed to accomplish our goals. For example, with the Activity Management System, one decides if the pursuit of a goal or an objective requires "an expenditure" of result time or of amorphous time - (usually) ahead of the engagement of time needed to accomplish that goal or objective. Afterwards, the goal-setter can better assess the quality of time devoted to the pursuit of the goal. And, when there are questions about whether time was wasted or not, the goal-setter can reference the type of time expended and any nesting effect for the time consumed in the pursuit of the activity (ies). Additionally, the goal-setter has a Goal Grid (assignment) for that activity. Also, with the vetting done via the Goal Distillation tools – there will be little doubt as to the quality of time spent on a given activity.

I overcame my over-reliance on **time management** techniques – which entailed constantly trying to squeeze more tasks (**quantitative** vs. qualitative choices) into the same amount of available time each day. The Activity Management System along with the Goal Discovery and Distillation Process team up to help you (and me) decide which tasks further which goals and objectives and which tasks have a higher priority than other tasks.

By the way, I never succeeded in managing to speed up or slow down the hands of a clock and I did not meet anyone else who could.

Prospecting For Goal(s)

The following story entitled, "Three Feet from Gold", illustrates well the stories that I have been told about ventures that people have engaged in - sometimes over and over again, in pursuit of success.

We buy books, cds, dvds and we attend classes, workshops, and seminars with the aim of becoming successful - even financially independent. But, after the stimulus, we revert to the old way - with another rock in our knapsack - weighing us down or discouraging us from taking another foolish foray into the elusive end state referred to as success.

THREE FEET FROM GOLD
Anonymous

One of the most common causes of failure is the habit of quitting when one is overtaken by "temporary defeat". Every person is guilty of this mistake at one time or another.

An uncle of R.U. Darby was caught by the "gold fever" in the gold-rush days and went west to dig and grow rich. He had never heard that "more gold has been mined from the thoughts of men than has ever been taken from the earth". He staked a claim and went to work with pick and shovel.

After weeks of labor, he was rewarded by the discovery of the shining ore. He needed machinery to bring the ore to the surface. Quietly, he covered up the mine, retraced his footsteps to his home in Williamsburg, Maryland, told his relatives and a few neighbors of the "strike". They got together money for the needed machinery and had it shipped. The uncle and Darby went back to work the mine.

The first car of ore was mined and shipped to a smelter. The returns proved they had one of the riches mines in Colorado! A few more cars of that ore would clear the debts. Then, would come the big killing in profits. Down went the drills! Up went the hopes of Darby and Uncle!

Then...something happened.

The vein of gold ore disappeared! They had come to the end of the rainbow and the pot of gold was no longer there. They drilled on, desperately trying to pick up the vein again - all to no avail.

FINALLY, they decided to QUIT.

They sold the machinery to a junk man for a few hundred dollars, and took the train back home.

The junk man called in a mining engineer to look at the mine and do a little calculating. The engineer advised that the project had failed because the owners were not familiar with "fault lines." His calculations showed that the vein would be found *JUST THREE FEET FROM WHERE THE DARBYS HAD STOPPED DRILLING!*

That is exactly where it was found. The junk man took millions of dollars in ore from the mine... because...He knew enough to seek expert counsel before giving up.

What is the moral of the story? Opportunities are **NEVER** lost... Just found by someone else.

This workbook could become another journey that lands you three feet from your gold (goals). Or, it can be the catalyst which helps you to realize the dreams and goals that you carry. The key is the emphasis on WORK in workbook. It is no quick task - getting through the worksheets, discovering, and distilling your goals. But, one must choose a vehicle, method, or process whereby she dedicates her time, energy, belief, and desire to accomplish that which is important to her. **NOW** is perpetual - it will always be **NOW** for you - **do it NOW!**

Don't forget that the simple reading of this workbook is doing it, but the doing of it also entails completing the worksheets and applying what you glean from this workbook to your benefit and the benefit of others who are significant to you.

What's Next?

The Goal Tree, The Goal Grid, and The Goal Circles exercises, in the next two chapters, will help you to begin the process of listing, evaluating, and prioritizing your wants and needs. And, as you become even more expert on you, you will discover that:

This world must conform to your picture of you!!!

Musing RE: *Nesting Awareness Quotient*

Musing RE: *Transition Awareness Quotient*

Musing RE: *What type of time is Activity Management?*

A future version of this workbook will contain a means of helping people become more aware of the nesting relationships that they find themselves in. With this knowledge, an individual can make more informed choices regarding the usage of her time. She can also help others to extricate themselves from situations that consume far too much time.

I believe that one or more readers will read this statement and develop a convenient solution to capturing (measuring) the time that is spent in a host of transitional activities throughout our days and lives.

Is transition time nested in another form of activity management? Can other forms of activity management be nested in transition time? These are just a couple of the questions which result from the usage of the activity management system - many others remain.

What type of time is activity management? Is it result time? Yes, as one typically works towards a result. Is it event time? Probably not, as the participant plays an active role in the creation of the individual strategic plan. Is it emergency time? In some cases it may be as life's circumstances can change dramatically - in moments.

Is it found time? On occasion, the time devoted to activity management may be the result of time freeing up, elsewhere (the exception). Is it amorphous time? This may be the best answer for many people as there is no set time for its completion. And, just because a plan is committed to a written form, doesn't mean that it is completed.

Is it unstructured time? By definition, no. However, one may choose to leave the unstructured time environment and work on her plan. And finally, is it transition time? There may be times that we think about our activity management and/or individual strategic plans while in transition from one state to another, but activity management typically resides in a given state.

Chapter 3 - Goal Mining Part 1 - Goal Discovery

- Other Goal Setting Systems
- Assumptions about Goals
- One Wish
- Tried and True Goal Setting Systems
- What Becomes A Goal?
- Goal Tree
- The Fruit of the Goal Tree

Other Goal Setting Systems

There are a great number of helpful tools on goal setting and planning for individuals, teams, and for organizations. One of the shortcomings of some of the books and articles on these topics is the lack of definition of the terms that the source uses to direct the efforts of the reader or adherent to the system(s) offered in the book or article. For example, terms such as goal and objective are used interchangeably in some reference books. And, vision and mission are also used interchangeably. Perhaps, the author is discussing a purpose or aim. One might ask what are the differences between a goal and an objective? One might then go to a reference book to obtain some clarity on the topic. But, in my experience, reference books do not provide clarity on the definitions as one term is sometimes used in the definition of the other. That lack of clarity extends to terms such as goal and objective, vision and mission, or aim and purpose.

To help you to get past this potential obstacle, I have provided working definitions [under the section on what becomes a goal, below] for the terms: vision, mission, plan, goal, objective, task, and result or desired outcome.

Assumptions about Goals

Have you ever been told to write down a goal or goals and cross them off your list once it is/they are accomplished? This could be sage advice, if:

1. you know what a goal is
2. you can translate the goal into do-able steps
3. you can access resources to help in your goal completion
4. you can remove obstacles and/or conflicts to your goal completion
5. you believe in your ability to accomplish the goal
6. you are willing to expend the effort for your goal completion
7. you really need to (or want to) accomplish the goal

Telling someone to set or accomplish a goal may not create a picture of the desired outcome or end result (for them) that you have in mind. My wife once told our son, who she wanted to cease a certain behavior, to cut it out (or stop). He left the room for a moment or two and returned with a small piece of paper with the word "it" written on it - he had cut that word out of a larger piece of paper. Therefore, my wife literally and figuratively got what she wanted - if only for a few moments. Our son left the room, ceasing the objectionable behavior (temporarily) and returned with the word "it" written on it cut out, as she had inadvertently asked him do.

One Wish

I am uncertain as to the origin of the story that I am about to tell. The scenario, as I recall, was similar to the scenarios popularized in Aesop's Fables. The story is about a very old man who contemplates his death and is overcome by a desire to return to the land of his youth. In those days, he may have lived no more than 20-30 miles from where he was raised. For the sake of the story, let's call him, Jaleel.

Jaleel is now a very old man who is also blind, a beggar, and he has one leg that is 1-2 inches shorter than the other causing him to limp when he walked. Jaleel's journey home was very strenuous for him. As he approached the village of his youth, he could hear sounds of people and livestock off in the distance. But, he was too tired to continue, so he rested for a time - falling asleep, briefly. As he awoke, he felt around for his few belongings - near his bare feet, he felt a warm object. He picked it up and held it close. In an attempt to warm his hands, he rubbed it vigorously. And, a genie popped out of the lantern that he held.

The genie said to Jaleel, I will grant you one wish and one wish only. The genie then said think slowly and carefully before making your (one) wish. OK, let's suppose that you are in Jaleel's place, what would you wish for?

- A longer life
- Better health
- Your vision
- Money
- Friends
- Your youth
- A companion

Or perhaps, you would wish for something else, entirely. Here is what Jaleel said to the genie:

I wish to live to see my great grandchildren's grandchildren-so that I may run, jump and play with them in their parent's great castle with its many rooms and loyal servants who attend to our every need!

In terms of Jaleel's former state (i.e. pre-wish), what problems were overcome via his **Omni-wish?** Yes, Omni-Wish, let's list a few:

- he lives to see his grandchildren extends his life by generations
- his blindness is gone
- running, jumping, and playing indicate a healthier state for Jaleel a castle and loyal servants indicate a degree of wealth
- living with his child (and her or his children) indicates a familial bond

Let's now look at a poem, from Napoleon Hill's "Think and Grow Rich".

"My Wage"
by Jessie B. Rittenhouse

"I bargained with Life for a penny,
And Life would pay no more,
However I begged at evening
When I counted my scanty store.
For Life is a just employer,
He gives you what you ask,
But once you have set the wages,
Why, you must bear the task.
I worked for a menial's hire,
Only to learn, dismayed,
That any wage I had asked of Life,
Life would have willingly paid."

In both instances, the individual at the center of the story and poem achieved a good deal less than he was capable of. Jaleel's fulfillment was realized via an **Omni-wish,** a holistic vision and desire for its fulfillment. Rittenhouse's character learned the lesson(s) of abundance via toil and introspection. The outcomes are more alike in terms of the insights by the respective characters. We do not have to wait for the omnipresent genie to come into our life to grant us our heart's desire. And, we do not have to wait until the end of our days for the brilliant insight of Rittenhouse. Remember, **NOW** is perpetual - therein is its power.

As long as there is breath in your body, you can call forth your genie to grant you the desired outcomes you seek or long for. If you have not yet decided what you want most in this life - we will cover how to determine that desire in the next chapter. And, if you have given up on your dream, you may also be able to re-link yourself to that dream in these pages.

Tried And True Goal Setting Systems

Write It Down

Each of the following goal setting systems has worked for me - to a point. However, due to my analytical nature, I constantly sought more information regarding the what, why, and how of goal setting success.

The first goal setting system or technique that I was exposed to was a simple write it (the goal) down on paper and cross it off when it was done approach. The fact that I had published my goal by committing it to paper may have been the motivation to accomplish it, but I am not really certain that was the reason I accomplished different goals using this technique.

I was told that Yale University published a longitudinal (over a number of years) study on goal setting. The results indicated the 3% of the people who wrote down their goals accomplished more than the 97% of the people who did not. Who wouldn't want to be part of that 3% elite of goal getters? Maybe, that was my motivation for achieving certain goals.

By the way, that Yale study is an urban legend, untrue. I wrote the school to ask about the study and to purchase a copy of the findings to share in workshops that I conducted. But, I was informed (in writing) that no such study had ever been done by them.

Rehearse and Celebrate

I consider myself quite fortunate to have taken many of the premier self-development training programs in existence. Some of these events were developed and/or conducted by the co-founder (along with his wife, Diane) of Seattle's The Pacific Institute, Lou Tice.

The gist of this marvelous goal setting technique is that one rehearses a desired outcome or scenario, mentally. When the rehearsal features the end result that you want, you celebrate that desired outcome, emotionally. You begin to act as if that event has already or is currently happening. You imbue your images with feelings of joy and enthusiasm - you also bring into play other senses besides vision, you must also "smell the smells", "taste the tastes", "hear the sounds", etc. until the images are alive and real - happening now – in your mind.

Young children are masterful at this technique. I recall watching my three children burst into celebration on days that I would come home and announce that we were going out for, drum roll please, pizza. They began to jump up and down-yelling Chuckie Cheese, Chuckie Cheese, Chuckie Cheese until we left in the car for Chuckie Cheese. They would take the steps needed to make this journey, i.e. washing their faces, going to the bathroom, changing clothes - when necessary - all on their own just to visit Chuckie Cheese and play on the toys.

Children immerse themselves in the wonderment of the event even prior to the actual occurrence of the event. How did we lose this sense of awe? When did we lose it? It may surprise you when I say that we have not lost it. We grown-ups, simply act our age, but put us in a room or place with a small child (or sometimes a pet), and that inner child springs forward regardless of the grown-ups' chronological age.

My grandmother was wheelchair-bound and nearly blind during her last few years of life. But, when I brought my daughter who was about six months old to see her (and grandpa who lived in a nursing home), she immediately perked up and became radiant as she held and talked with her great grand-daughter. As my grandparents were married 75 years when they died, they had seen more than two dozen grandchildren and many great grandchildren so it was not the novelty of seeing a great grandchild, but rather a natural exuberance brought about in the presence of a new life and all the promise that it holds, grandma would be so proud if she could see her great granddaughter now.

C+B=A

A co-worker once invited me to an Amway meeting. One of the most compelling reasons for attending future meetings was the focus on self-help and personal development via workshops and books and tapes. Especially, helpful was the Napoleon Hill book, "Think and Grow Rich", which I read and re-read (along with other writings by Hill). The poem, above, concerning bargaining with life for a penny, struck a responsive chord with me as it reflected choice into the equation of our lives.

At an Amway seminar, a speaker said words to the effect whatever the mind of man can conceive and believe it can achieve. Stated another way, Conceive + Believe = Achieve, hence C+B=A. And, for a time, this equation became my goal-setting mantra.

5-Step Goal Formula

I have seen at least three variations of the following goal setting formula in use in various business trainings. Briefly, it states that goal setting is comprised of the following components, goals are written in:

1. **The first person**, singular - plural only if each person consents to "we"
2. **Present tense**, i.e. NOW rather than "will"
3. **Specific** if you want more money and I offer you a dime you would have more money. But, if you state that you have a net worth of one million dollars that is specific - more money is not specific.

4. **Measurable** desiring more education is not measurable until you make it specific such as I now have my PMP in project management, i.e. its professional certification. Progress toward and the receipt of the certification are all measurable.
5. **Time Limit** before I am too old to enjoy it is not a good yardstick or time limit. But to say that by my next, 40th or 50th birthday or by my 3rd or 5th year at this job, I see myself managing...

People, everywhere, have made these and other goal-setting systems work. But, not without the WORK - the belief in the desirability of or need for the desired outcome - so can you - with this workbook!

Pseudo-Goals

There really is value in each of the foregoing goal setting system as not having a goal setting system or technique exposes one to the following type of statements or beliefs as surrogates for real goal statements:

1. I am not going to be like my dad
2. I am going to college
3. I want to get married

The hazard in what I call pseudo-goals is that they are not specific or measurable, etc. They can even lead to an opposite result. For example, statement #1 does not tell the reader what the speaker will be like or wishes to be like - if not like his dad [what was the dad like, anyway]. This statement even allows for the possibility that the one affirming it may end up worse than the dad, assuming that the dad had a character flaw, which the affirmer wanted to avoid. We must learn to eliminate the picturing or speaking into existence of things that we do not want as we are likely to move towards that which we picture - good or bad.

Statement #2, provides for a scenario wherein, one attends college for a day, week, or month and drops out. The college experience should result in the receipt of an earned degree or certificate in a field or practice that is rewarding to the recipient and her customers or employer. Statement #3, includes scenarios wherein the affirmer is unhappily married or abandoned. Most of us would agree that being happily married is preferable to just getting married. And, being happily married over many years is preferable to a brief marriage that sours or ends, tragically.

During a workshop that I conducted as a facilitator for The Pacific Institute, a participant came to me to obtain help with writing his affirmations. He was a new pilot and was doing what he called "touch and gos". In his affirmations he alluded to his prowess in taking off and maneuvering the plane, etc. I asked him if it was also important to have safe - even expert landings - to which he quickly agreed.

As a general rule, I suggest to anyone writing affirmations to always include the adverbs Safely, Happily, and Easily (SHE) in all her affirmations as it can take the edge off an affirmation that is not carefully screened in terms of the desired outcome(s).

Unspoken Goals

The problem with the Pseudo-goals, above, was that they were not specific and/or measurable. That lack of specificity also plagues Unspoken Goals. Examples include:

1. Why do I always end up with jerks...?
2. I don't know why I put up with your...
3. You are soooo stupid.

There is a great deal of excellent work on self-talk and self-speak. Dr. Shad Helmstetter and Mr. Lou Tice are the authors / speakers that I have, personally, benefitted the most from reading and listening to.

If we are not diligent in our practice of guarding our self-talk, self speak, along with what we allow others to say to us, we may derail our own progress. Let's look at the first statement, above, why do I always end up with jerks? What is not being said (among other things) is why do I attract people who mistreat me or why am I not worthy of a better mate or what is wrong with me that no one is interested in me - but the toxic kind of person that I always attract.

Statement #2, reveals a lot about the speaker as she seems to be saying - you are the best that I can do or I deserve you or why am I still with or attracted to you. Statement #3 hides the words - why do I want to or need to be with someone that I think is stupid (soooo stupid)? Our self-speak, (what we say out loud) often reveals what we really think or feel about ourselves - in a given situation.

If you use a different method of goal discovery, you still need a way to distill or reduce and prioritize the goals that you select. An, often times, overlooked step in other systems is the reduction of or removal of goal conflicts (Chapter 4). These goal conflicts can have the effect of stalling one's progress towards her goal(s) fulfillment.

What Becomes A Goal?

Before I attempt to answer that question, let's agree on the definitions that follow - if only for the time that it takes to complete this workbook. I once attended a meeting with close to forty people in attendance - virtually everyone there had a graduate degree or two. However, we had a disagreement as to what was a vision and what was a mission. Afterwards, I consulted six or seven reference books for definitions for the terms, below. But, there was no uniformity [or clarity] in terms of the definitions for these terms in those popular reference volumes. In fact, one word was sometimes used to define or describe another. Thus, my proffer of these definitions:

***Goals Mini-Glossary

Vision

A Strong Purpose + A Picture of the Desired or Required Outcome. Vision can be experienced as an idea or feeling regarding the desired outcome, which is held in mind and/or heart.

Mission

The objectification of or out-picturing of a Vision. Clothing of the vision begins here. A Mission is the Direction to or the Direction from one's Vision-based on one's present position. Thinking, Feeling, and Behaviors are channeled in a given direction(s).

Plan

A (written) statement of Goals, Objectives, Tasks, Resource + Options (Plan B, C, etc.) A plan answers the questions - who, what, why, where, when and how and it includes a SWOT Analysis and/or What if scenarios. Keyword: Assessment.

Goal

A thing to be obtained, given, shared, done or a state of being to be attained. During this step, Timetables and Milestones (Metrics) are developed.

Objective

A step to be taken to achieve or attain a goal.

Task

An activity that cannot be sub-divided any further in the attainment of an objective. To Do Items are typically Tasks.

End Result

The cumulative effect of the foregoing series of activities.

Desired Outcome

The Enriched Vision = The result planned for, hoped for, and towards which effort and resources are directed.

Strategy - Macro

Exercising forethought regarding the linking of each successive element of the Vision Continuum or Idea Realization Continuum [iterations of a vision] through to its end result.

Tactic - Micro

Exercising forethought regarding the execution of an element of the Vision Continuum.

*** These definitions are from my Idea Realization Continuum or Vision Continuum a heuristic planning tool that will be published at a future date.

So, what does become a goal? Perhaps, a parent who says do your homework before you go to (bed, school, out...) or a boss who says you will have to stay late the next couple of days until you get this project completed or you watch a commercial and see the perfect SUV or hybrid [or hybrid SUV] for your active family, but it is about $10,000 more than you had budgeted for a new vehicle; or your child wins a science, music or athletic scholarship to a university 2,500 miles from home; or you present a paper at a conference and you receive an offer of employment at double you current salary. Each of these scenarios can become a goal, but first one's vision of possible futures is changed/ expanded/ tweaked. From that new vision, one adjusts missions and plans yielding a new set of (dynamic the only kind of) goals.

Goal Discovery and Distillation

TOOL: Self-Image Grid(s)

USE: Discover Self-Images and Group Images Team/Group Images

The process of goal discovery need not be accidental or reactive as in the section on what becomes a goal, above. You can purposely explore needs and wants at the core of your being to determine what you desire most and need most to do, be, have, or share. You will (soon) be given tools to find those needs and wants as well as tools to help you prioritize and keep track of the accomplishment of your needs and wants.

One of these tools is The Self-Image Grid, which helps us to begin to see ourselves in a more complete way. For example, if we examine ourselves under a single category, such as an athlete. Some of us will excel in all things athletic, others will not. And, when we add student to this grid, some of us will excel in math, science, language, music, art, machine shop, photography, home economics, or computer hardware / or software development, others will not.

By the time we complete the list of topics, virtually all of us will find one or more topics that we can do well. I developed this form to help students in my self-esteem workshops as many of them believed that they had low self-esteem. This assessment was generalized to cover a wide range of endeavors. The fact is that I have never met an individual who had low self esteem in all parts of her or his life.

We all have one or more things that we do well or very well. By having another person complete a Self-Image Grid (for you) along with our own, you may begin to see yourself in a whole new light as a person with high or moderately high self-esteem, in a given area(s).

One of the great "aha" moments for students who completed this exercise is that they found out that they had multiple self-images - one for each activity or situation that they experienced. One finds that there are things that she excels in and things she does not excel in. And, the false conclusion that she had low self-esteem was proven to be incorrect - once the results of this exercise were obtained and analyzed, i.e. internalized.

After you complete this form, please consider using the blank form to incorporate the areas in your life that are important to you, e.g. being a parent, entrepreneur, speaker, dancer, student, employee, friend, volunteer, or retiree. Then assess yourself using those terms. Also, have another person assess you to compare results. The contents of the Self-Image Grid are solely up to the person(s) using it.

Once these steps are done, you begin the process of goal discovery and goal distillation by listing your dreams, loves, desires, and likes with the tools provided herein. And, list your shoulds, musts, have tos, and dislikes, which may become smaller, more manageable, and/or less stressful as a result of completing these exercises. The Self-image Grid will enlarge or enrich your sense of self and what you can do.

SELF-IMAGE

*Limits Vision

*Enlarges Vision

The Self-Image Grid

This form is an actual form from a workshop that I conducted. As the participants were from diverse backgrounds, we listed more things than the typical individual will list for her own Self-Image Grid. However, there is no reason why you cannot have more or fewer roles or characteristics in your Self-Image Grid - the choice is yours. I suggest that you place a minimum of 15-20 roles on your Self-Image Grid and evaluate each in terms of the scale of 1-10, with one being the lowest or "poor" to 10 being the highest or excellent.

PERSONAL STRATEGIC PLANNING										
SELF-IMAGE GRID										
	POOR				FAIR		GOOD		EXCELLENT	
SELF-IMAGE AS	1	2	3	4	5	6	7	8	9	10
Athlete:										
*Bowler										
*Golfer										
*Marathoner										
*Rock Climber										
*Skier										
*Sky Diver										
Child										
Cook										
Driver										
Employee										
Entrepreneur										
Friend										
Gardener										
Housekeeper										
Inventor										
Mate										
Parent										
Risk-taker										
Role Model										
Speaker										
Student										
TEAM:										
Athletic:										
Church										
Family										
Friendships										
Marriage										
Relationship										
School										
Work/Company										
MISC.										
Body										
Car										
City										
Home										
Wardrobe										
COPYRIGHT- James S. Gordon 1994-2011										

The Blank Self-Image Grid

The blank Self-Image Grid allows you to select roles or characteristics that are important to you. You may then assess yourself on the scale used, herein. Or, feel free to customize the content of this form.

SELF-IMAGE AS:	1	POOR 2	3	FAIR 4	5	6	GOOD 7	8	EXCELLENT 9	10
PERSONAL STRATEGIC PLANNING										
SELF-IMAGE GRID										
Athlete:										
TEAM:										
MISC.										
COPYRIGHT- James S. Gordon 1994-2017										

Self-Image Grid for Students

The final example is that of a high school (or college) student. This student's profile includes having her assess her first and subsequent class periods, throughout the day. There is also room for an assessment of extra-curricular activities and evening endeavors.

Please take a moment to write down other significant roles that you would like to gain more insight into. Each of those roles can be made to illustrate aspects, elements, or attributes associated with the role. You may use the blank forms contained in this workbook or create your own.

Each student should consult a trusted adult for insight into her assessment of herself - using the criteria of the student's School-Image Grid.

School-Image Grid

		PERSONAL STRATEGIC PLANNING									
		SELF-IMAGE GRID - School Version									
		POOR			FAIR		GOOD				EXCELLENT	
SELF-IMAGE AS:	1	2	3	4	5	6	7	8	9	10
Home: Mornings										
1st Period										
2nd Period										
3rd Period										
4th Period										
5th Period										
6th Period										
7th Period										
8th Period										
9th Period										
10th Period										
Extra-Curricular (EC)										
EC-1										
EC-2										
EC-3										
Home: Evenings										
Job - Present										
Job - Past 1										
Job - Past 2										
TEAM:										
Athletic										
Church										
Family										
Friends										
School										
MISC.										
Body										
Car										
Home										
Wardrobe										
					COPYRIGHT - James S Gordon				1994-2017	

TEAM-IMAGE

- How do we see one another?
- How well do we work together?
- What is our potential for success?

I have never met anyone that did not belong to some sort of team or group. Examples include: student, employee, soldier, spouse, sibling, neighbor, citizen, gender, age, etc. For those on teams, there are typical rankings in terms of wins and losses. For companies, oftentimes, there is market share or some other generally agreed upon metric that determines how we feel about the group or team or how well it performs.

People, sometimes, assess their marriage or family - comparing or contrasting it with other marriages or families. Using the Team Image Grid, we will assess different attributes of a team and what you think of your team or group on each attribute.

As with the Self-Image Grid, you will have a blank form that you can use to add meaningful attributes on which you can assess your team or group. And, you will find that teams and groups have multiple team- images based on the attribute being assessed. One assessor may rate the team high on an attribute and one or more others may rate the team lower in that same attribute.

TEAM-IMAGE	1	POER 2	3	4	FAIR 5	6	GOOD 7	8	EXCELLENT 9	10
PERSONAL STRATEGIC PLANNING										
TEAM-IMAGE GRID										
1. Accomplish Goals										
2. Cohesion										
3. Communication										
4. Competence										
5. Criticism										
6. Decision-Making										
7. Delegating										
8. Discipline										
9. Diversity										
10. Enthusiasm										
11. Experience										
12. Flexibility										
13. Humor										
14. Innovate										
15. Interaction										
16. Leadership										
17. Marketing										
18. Motivation										
19. Organization										
20. Planning										
21. Recognition										
22. Reliability										
23. Socialize										
24. Structure										
25. Technology										
26. Train/Mentor										
TEAMS (T):										
T1:										
T2:										
T3:										
T4:										
T5:										
T6:										
T7:										
T8:										
T9:										
T10:										
COPYRIGHT- James S. Gordon 1994-2011										

43

Goal Tree:

TOOL: Goal Tree
USE: Identifies and Separates Needs and Wants

Our Goal Tree is comprised of eight branches, the respective branches are: dreams, loves, likes, agrees to, avoids, musts, shoulds, agrees (not to). Please take the time to list at least three to five responses for each category. If you are stuck at one or two responses, go on to the next category. And, if more responses occur to you later – add them to this exercise. These inputs will carry over to the next stage of the Goal Distillation Process, the Goal Grid.

Goal Tree Exercise

Dream - The thing that you would do if you only had enough time, money, courage, freedom, etc. Don't pre-judge the dream as being unlikely or impossible, simply list it for now.

    1. _____
    2. _____
    3. _____
    4. _____
    5. _____

Questions:

A. **Whose idea is this activity?** Did someone else suggest, recommend, or demand that you do this activity?

B. **Why do it?** What do you gain or attain as a result of completing this activity?

C. **To be done by/ with whom?** Can you do it alone or are others needed to accomplish the activity?

D. **How is it to be done?** Is there a prescribed manner in which this activity must be done?

E. **What is to be done?** What are the discreet tasks that are to be accomplished? Is an action plan or project plan needed to accomplish the activity?

F. **When is it to be done?** Is there a deadline to start and/or complete the activity? Is there a schedule or is a schedule needed for its completion?

G. **Where is it to be done?** Though a tad far-fetched, a commencement address, a rodeo, sky-diving, or a skate party cannot be done, anywhere location can be critical to the success of the undertaking.

H. **If not done-what happens?** Just how urgent (if at all) is the activity? What are the consequences of not doing it? Can you live with that outcome? If not, why not?

I. **When done-what happens?** If you have not yet done this activity, what do you imagine to be the benefits of doing the activity? Does this outcome place you closer to or further from your goal?

J. **How do you feel about that?** Satisfied, proud, excited, joyful, relieved, sad, other?

K. **Will you do this activity again**? Why or why not?

Love - The things that truly excite and motivate you when you are doing it or thinking about doing it, again.

    1. _____
    2. _____
    3. _____
    4. _____
    5. _____

Questions:

A. **Whose idea is this activity?** Did someone else suggest, recommend, or demand that you do this activity?

B. **Why do it?** What do you gain or attain as a result of completing this activity?

C. **To be done by/ with whom?** Can you do it alone or are others needed to accomplish the activity?

D. **How is it to be done?** Is there a prescribed manner in which this activity must be done?

E. **What is to be done?** What are the discreet tasks that are to be accomplished? Is an action plan or project plan needed to accomplish the activity?

F. **When is it to be done?** Is there a deadline to start and/or complete the activity? Is there a schedule or is a schedule needed for its completion?

G. **Where is it to be done?** Though a tad far-fetched, a commencement address, a rodeo, sky-diving, or a skate party cannot be done, anywhere location can be critical to the success of the undertaking.

H. **If not done-what happens?** Just how urgent (if at all) is the activity? What are the consequences of not doing it? Can you live with that outcome? If not, why not?

I. **When done-what happens?** If you have not yet done this activity, what do you imagine to be the benefits of doing the activity? Does this outcome place you closer to or further from your goal?

J. **How do you feel about that?** Satisfied, proud, excited, joyful, relieved, sad, other?

K. **Will you do this activity again**? Why or why not?

Like - These things are done when you are being sociable, neighborly, or a helping hand.

    1. _____
    2. _____
    3. _____
    4. _____
    5. _____

Questions:

A. **Whose idea is this activity?** Did someone else suggest, recommend, or demand that you do this activity?

B. **Why do it?** What do you gain or attain as a result of completing this activity?

C. **To be done by/ with whom?** Can you do it alone or are others needed to accomplish the activity?

D. **How is it to be done?** Is there a prescribed manner in which this activity must be done?

E. **What is to be done?** What are the discreet tasks that are to be accomplished? Is an action plan or project plan needed to accomplish the activity?

F. **When is it to be done?** Is there a deadline to start and/or complete the activity? Is there a schedule or is a schedule needed for its completion?

G. **Where is it to be done?** Though a tad far-fetched, a commencement address, a rodeo, sky-diving, or a skate party cannot be done, anywhere location can be critical to the success of the undertaking.

H. **If not done-what happens?** Just how urgent (if at all) is the activity? What are the consequences of not doing it? Can you live with that outcome? If not, why not?

I. **When done-what happens?** If you have not yet done this activity, what do you imagine to be the benefits of doing the activity? Does this outcome place you closer to or further from your goal?

J. **How do you feel about that?** Satisfied, proud, excited, joyful, relieved, sad, other?

K. **Will you do this activity again**? Why or why not?

Agree 1 - These things you might not do on your own, but often are the "quid pro quos" of life... one might say, I was bored so we went to the movie, shopping, play miniature golf...

1. _____
2. _____
3. _____
4. _____
5. _____

Questions:

A. **Whose idea is this activity?** Did someone else suggest, recommend, or demand that you do this activity?

B. **Why do it?** What do you gain or attain as a result of completing this activity?

C. **To be done by/ with whom?** Can you do it alone or are others needed to accomplish the activity?

D. **How is it to be done?** Is there a prescribed manner in which this activity must be done?

E. **What is to be done?** What are the discreet tasks that are to be accomplished? Is an action plan or project plan needed to accomplish the activity?

F. **When is it to be done?** Is there a deadline to start and/or complete the activity? Is there a schedule or is a schedule needed for its completion?

G. **Where is it to be done?** Though a tad far-fetched, a commencement address, a rodeo, sky-diving, or a skate party cannot be done, anywhere location can be critical to the success of the undertaking.

H. **If not done-what happens?** Just how urgent (if at all) is the activity? What are the consequences of not doing it? Can you live with that outcome? If not, why not?

I. **When done-what happens?** If you have not yet done this activity, what do you imagine to be the benefits of doing the activity? Does this outcome place you closer to or further from your goal?

J. **How do you feel about that?** Satisfied, proud, excited, joyful, relieved, sad, other?

K. **Will you do this activity again**? Why or why not?

Avoid - Things that you go out of your way to avoid doing...even "vow" to not do or not do, again.

1. _____
2. _____
3. _____
4. _____
5. _____

Questions:

A. **Whose idea is this activity?** Did someone else suggest, recommend, or demand that you do this activity?

B. **Why do it?** What do you gain or attain as a result of completing this activity?

C. **To be done by/ with whom?** Can you do it alone or are others needed to accomplish the activity?

D. **How is it to be done?** Is there a prescribed manner in which this activity must be done?

E. **What is to be done?** What are the discreet tasks that are to be accomplished? Is an action plan or project plan needed to accomplish the activity?

F. **When is it to be done?** Is there a deadline to start and/or complete the activity? Is there a schedule or is a schedule needed for its completion?

G. **Where is it to be done?** Though a tad far-fetched, a commencement address, a rodeo, sky-diving, or a skate party cannot be done, anywhere location can be critical to the success of the undertaking.

H. **If not done-what happens?** Just how urgent (if at all) is the activity? What are the consequences of not doing it? Can you live with that outcome? If not, why not?

I. **When done-what happens?** If you have not yet done this activity, what do you imagine to be the benefits of doing the activity? Does this outcome place you closer to or further from your goal?

J. **How do you feel about that?** Satisfied, proud, excited, joyful, relieved, sad, other?

K. **Will you do this activity again**? Why or why not?

Must - Things that you are forced or coerced into...an unpleasant task at work, a court-ordered matter.

1. _____
2. _____
3. _____
4. _____
5. _____

Questions:

A. **Whose idea is this activity?** Did someone else suggest, recommend, or demand that you do this activity?

B. **Why do it?** What do you gain or attain as a result of completing this activity?

C. **To be done by/ with whom?** Can you do it alone or are others needed to accomplish the activity?

D. **How is it to be done?** Is there a prescribed manner in which this activity must be done?

E. **What is to be done?** What are the discreet tasks that are to be accomplished? Is an action plan or project plan needed to accomplish the activity?

F. **When is it to be done?** Is there a deadline to start and/or complete the activity? Is there a schedule or is a schedule needed for its completion?

G. **Where is it to be done?** Though a tad far-fetched, a commencement address, a rodeo, sky-diving, or a skate party cannot be done, anywhere location can be critical to the success of the undertaking.

H. **If not done-what happens?** Just how urgent (if at all) is the activity? What are the consequences of not doing it? Can you live with that outcome? If not, why not?

I. **When done-what happens?** If you have not yet done this activity, what do you imagine to be the benefits of doing the activity? Does this outcome place you closer to or further from your goal?

J. **How do you feel about that?** Satisfied, proud, excited, joyful, relieved, sad, other?

K. **Will you do this activity again**? Why or why not?

Should - Things that you should do (according to conscience or custom) - whether or not you are actually doing them.

    1. _____
    2. _____
    3. _____

4. _____
5. _____

Questions:

A. **Whose idea is this activity?** Did someone else suggest, recommend, or demand that you do this activity?

B. **Why do it?** What do you gain or attain as a result of completing this activity?

C. **To be done by/ with whom?** Can you do it alone or are others needed to accomplish the activity?

D. **How is it to be done?** Is there a prescribed manner in which this activity must be done?

E. **What is to be done?** What are the discreet tasks that are to be accomplished? Is an action plan or project plan needed to accomplish the activity?

F. **When is it to be done?** Is there a deadline to start and/or complete the activity? Is there a schedule or is a schedule needed for its completion?

G. **Where is it to be done?** Though a tad far-fetched, a commencement address, a rodeo, sky-diving, or a skate party cannot be done, anywhere location can be critical to the success of the undertaking.

H. **If not done-what happens?** Just how urgent (if at all) is the activity? What are the consequences of not doing it? Can you live with that outcome? If not, why not?

I. **When done-what happens?** If you have not yet done this activity, what do you imagine to be the benefits of doing the activity? Does this outcome place you closer to or further from your goal?

J. **How do you feel about that?** Satisfied, proud, excited, joyful, relieved, sad, other?

K. **Will you do this activity again**? Why or why not?

Agree-2 - Things that you agree to do but want to get out of, immediately and passionately...

1. _____
2. _____
3. _____
4. _____
5. _____

Questions:

A. **Whose idea is this activity?** Did someone else suggest, recommend, or demand that you do this activity?

B. **Why do it?** What do you gain or attain as a result of completing this activity?

C. **To be done by/ with whom?** Can you do it alone or are others needed to accomplish the activity?

D. **How is it to be done?** Is there a prescribed manner in which this activity must be done?

E. **What is to be done?** What are the discreet tasks that are to be accomplished? Is an action plan or project plan needed to accomplish the activity?

F. **When is it to be done?** Is there a deadline to start and/or complete the activity? Is there a schedule or is a schedule needed for its completion?

G. **Where is it to be done?** Though a tad far-fetched, a commencement address, a rodeo, sky-diving, or a skate party cannot be done, anywhere location can be critical to the success of the undertaking.

H. **If not done-what happens?** Just how urgent (if at all) is the activity? What are the consequences of not doing it? Can you live with that outcome? If not, why not?

I. **When done-what happens?** If you have not yet done this activity, what do you imagine to be the benefits of doing the activity? Does this outcome place you closer to or further from your goal?

J. **How do you feel about that?** Satisfied, proud, excited, joyful, relieved, sad, other?

K. **Will you do this activity again**? Why or why not?

The Fruit of the Goal Tree

Now that you have compiled all of this information, what do you do, next? The Goal Tree activity helps us to outline our needs and wants. We are, now, taking an initial snapshot of our thinking and feelings on wants and needs. Over time, you will refine these target areas for your individual strategic plan.

The output from your goal discovery exercise will be placed in our Goal Distillation tools, i.e. the Goal Grid and the Goal Circles, then the Linked To Do List. With these tools you will be able to choose your priorities. Then, you can resolve conflicts amongst your goals and/or with others' goals. You will also expand or perfect your definition of success. Combined, you will have the tools to discover, distill, and create the goals, which are congruent with your definition of success.

Musing RE: *Need vs. Want Motivation Quotient*

How nice it would be to be able to measure the strength of one's needs versus one's wants. How can we best reduce conflict between our needs and our wants? Am I more successful when I work from a needs basis or a wants basis?

Is it more important to work from a needs basis or a wants basis? Which basis is a better forecast of success? Which basis is a better forecast of failure?

Chapter 4, Goal Mining - Part 2, The Goal Distillation Process

- Goal Grid
- Goal Conflicts
- Goal Circles
- Linked To Do List

Goal Grid Inputs

TOOL: Goal Grid
USE: Prioritize goals

Guidelines:

List things that you would like to have/ do/ become under each goal "topic". **These inputs are to be taken from the Goal Tree lists that you have just completed.** Place the two-letter abbreviations (Goal Grid Elements, which follow this diagram) that appear in parentheses ( ) inside the Goal Grid. For example, Family goal #1 (FA1) may be placed (as an example only) in the spot "10/10" in the grid, whereas Social goal #3 (SO3) may be at "5/5". You may add goals or use less than the spaces provided as there is no set amount of goals an individual can or "should" have. And, only you can determine the respective intensity of each need or each want.

The "X" axis represents the need priority you attribute to this goal's accomplishment. The "Y" axis represents the intensity of your desire to accomplish the goal.

The Goal Grid

The Goal Grid

WANT TO DO

		1	2	3	4	5	6	7	8	9	10
N	1										
E	2										
E	3										
D	4										
	5										
T	6										
O	7										
	8										
D	9										
O	10										

Again, this graph will illustrate our desire and need **intensity** on a low to high basis. Let's say that you have five career oriented dreams, desires, or goals - numbered (CA1), (CA2), (CA3), (CA4), and (CA5). You would place each one in a spot in this matrix which indicates how much you want and how urgently you need to experience the goal. It is okay if your desire for an aspect of your career to be more intense than the perceived need intensity you experience or vice versa.

This exercise simply gives you a snapshot of your current profile. When you re-visit these goals on the interval of time that you select, your perception may have changed as to the placement of one goal versus another goal.

Please list a Goal Grid Element, e.g. CA1 of FA1 - then circle or underline whether the following elements are want tos, choose tos, need tos, or have tos – in the exercise, which follows the display of the Goal Grid Elements.

Goal Grid Elements

- Career (CA)
- Community (CO)
- Education (ED)
- Family (FA)
- Health Physical (HP)
- Health Mental (HM)
- Marriage (MA)
- Personal (PE)
- Social (SO)
- Spiritual (SP)
- Other 1 (OT)
- Other 2 (OT)
- Other 3 (OT)
- Other 4 (OT)

Career (CA)

1. _____Want To/Choose To/Need To/Have To
2. _____Want To/Choose To/Need To/Have To
3. _____Want To/Choose To/Need To/Have To
4. _____Want To/Choose To/Need To/Have To
5. _____Want To/Choose To/Need To/Have To

Community (CO)

1. _____Want To/Choose To/Need To/Have To
2. _____Want To/Choose To/Need To/Have To
3. _____Want To/Choose To/Need To/Have To
4. _____Want To/Choose To/Need To/Have To
5. _____Want To/Choose To/Need To/Have To

Education (ED)

1. _____Want To/Choose To/Need To/Have To
2. _____Want To/Choose To/Need To/Have To
3. _____Want To/Choose To/Need To/Have To
4. _____Want To/Choose To/Need To/Have To
5. _____Want To/Choose To/Need To/Have To

Family (FA)

1. _____Want To/Choose To/Need To/Have To
2. _____Want To/Choose To/Need To/Have To
3. _____Want To/Choose To/Need To/Have To
4. _____Want To/Choose To/Need To/Have To
5. _____Want To/Choose To/Need To/Have To

Health Physical (HP)

1. _____Want To/Choose To/Need To/Have To
2. _____Want To/Choose To/Need To/Have To
3. _____Want To/Choose To/Need To/Have To
4. _____Want To/Choose To/Need To/Have To
5. _____Want To/Choose To/Need To/Have To

Health Mental (HM)

1. _____Want To/Choose To/Need To/Have To
2. _____Want To/Choose To/Need To/Have To
3. _____Want To/Choose To/Need To/Have To
4. _____Want To/Choose To/Need To/Have To
5. _____Want To/Choose To/Need To/Have To

Marriage (MA)

1. _____Want To/Choose To/Need To/Have To

2. _____Want To/Choose To/Need To/Have To
3. _____Want To/Choose To/Need To/Have To
4. _____Want To/Choose To/Need To/Have To
5. _____Want To/Choose To/Need To/Have To

Personal (PE)

1. _____Want To/Choose To/Need To/Have To
2. _____Want To/Choose To/Need To/Have To
3. _____Want To/Choose To/Need To/Have To
4. _____Want To/Choose To/Need To/Have To
5. _____Want To/Choose To/Need To/Have To

Social (SO)

1. _____Want To/Choose To/Need To/Have To
2. _____Want To/Choose To/Need To/Have To
3. _____Want To/Choose To/Need To/Have To
4. _____Want To/Choose To/Need To/Have To
5. _____Want To/Choose To/Need To/Have To

Spiritual (SP)

1. _____Want To/Choose To/Need To/Have To
2. _____Want To/Choose To/Need To/Have To
3. _____Want To/Choose To/Need To/Have To
4. _____Want To/Choose To/Need To/Have To
5. _____Want To/Choose To/Need To/Have To

Other 1 (OT 1)

1. _____Want To/Choose To/Need To/Have To
2. _____Want To/Choose To/Need To/Have To
3. _____Want To/Choose To/Need To/Have To
4. _____Want To/Choose To/Need To/Have To
5. _____Want To/Choose To/Need To/Have To

Other 2 (OT 2)

1. _____Want To/Choose To/Need To/Have To
2. _____Want To/Choose To/Need To/Have To
3. _____Want To/Choose To/Need To/Have To
4. _____Want To/Choose To/Need To/Have To
5. _____Want To/Choose To/Need To/Have To

Other 3 (OT 3)

1. _____Want To/Choose To/Need To/Have To
2. _____Want To/Choose To/Need To/Have To
3. _____Want To/Choose To/Need To/Have To
4. _____Want To/Choose To/Need To/Have To
5. _____Want To/Choose To/Need To/Have To

Other 4 (OT 4)

1. _____Want To/Choose To/Need To/Have To
2. _____Want To/Choose To/Need To/Have To
3. _____Want To/Choose To/Need To/Have To
4. _____Want To/Choose To/Need To/Have To
5. _____Want To/Choose To/Need To/Have To

Goal Conflicts

TOOL: Goal Circles

USE: Reduce goal conflicts by coordinating interpersonal and intrapersonal goals

Guidelines: Take each Goal Grid topic area and examine the objectives that you have written. Compare and contrast your "want tos" and "have tos" with those of your significant other, job's or among your own goals (one goal vs. another goal). The criteria include an inferior relationship, an equal relationship, and a superior relationship. There is another orientation called "Integrated" (or merged), wherein one goal partially or fully incorporates the (an)other('s) goal. This notion is suggested in "all work and no play" comments or one being referred to as a "workaholic". And, we see an integrated or merged orientation in parents who forego personal pursuits as they help their children obtain every possible advantage.

Determine what orientation (inferior, equal, superior, or integrated) one goal has vs. the other goal; and ask yourself or your significant other if that relationship is satisfactory. If it is not satisfactory, make an adjustment / compromise to reach a solution.

We can examine a number of situations with this tool, e.g. "my desire" is greater than or less than or equal to "your desire" or "your need" is greater than or less than or equal to "my need"; we can also look at other permutations of these relationships. In each case, determine whether the "relationship" between the goals is less than, equal to, greater than... we are not judging whether the relationship is good or bad, but rather observing the relationship in terms of more, less or equal in *INTENSITY AND/OR PRIORITY* to another goal or another's goal(s). And, we are assessing the degree of satisfaction or lack thereof that we have with that "state".

Goal Circles

Please consider keeping goals that are career oriented together with career oriented goals - at first. On one or more subsequent passes you can compare and contrast goals in other areas of your life, e.g. social or community perhaps, even family. The order is up to you to determine what works best.

Again, it is up to you to determine if you wish to compare or contrast your own goals one against another using the Goal Circles or you may compare or contrast your goals with your significant other's goals or you may choose to compare or contrast your goals with your employer's or co-worker's goals. Or, you may opt to do all of the above.

This process helps you to discover which goals get your immediate attention and which goals go on the proverbial "back burner". And, the process will provide you with insights into areas that are in conflict with intra-personal or inter-personal goals.

INDIVIDUAL STRATEGIC PLANNING
w/Goal Distillation Process

GOAL CIRCLES

GOAL ORIENTATION ANALYSIS	LIST GOALS FROM GOAL GRID
Equal — MINE, YOURS / OURS	
Superior — MINE, YOURS **or** MINE / YOURS	
Inferior — MINE, YOURS **or** YOURS / MINE	
Integrated — MINE YOURS / YOURS MINE	

COPYRIGHT- James S. Gordon 1978-2011

Daily Tasks

TOOL: Linked To Do List

USE: Organize daily activities

Guidelines:

List the tasks that you choose to accomplish each day on the line following the numbers 1-10. When that task is completed, check the box following the task. Next, circle the letter **U** if the task was unplanned or circle the **P** if the task was planned. After the notation **Grid#**, list the Goal Grid # for the task that you completed, e.g. CO1, ED2, FA1, etc. In this way, you can track whether the things that you do are aligned with needs, wants, or neither...

Linked To Do List

TO DO LIST – Mon-Fri

1. _____; **U/P; Grid#____**
2. _____; **U/P; Grid#____**
3. _____; **U/P; Grid#____**
4. _____; **U/P; Grid#____**
5. _____; **U/P; Grid#____**
6. _____; **U/P; Grid#____**
7. _____; **U/P; Grid#____**
8. _____; **U/P; Grid#____**
9. _____; **U/P; Grid#____**
10. _____; **U/P; Grid#____**

1. _____; **U/P; Grid#____**
2. _____; **U/P; Grid#____**
3. _____; **U/P; Grid#____**
4. _____; **U/P; Grid#____**
5. _____; **U/P; Grid#____**
6. _____; **U/P; Grid#____**
7. _____; **U/P; Grid#____**
8. _____; **U/P; Grid#____**
9. _____; **U/P; Grid#____**
10. _____; **U/P; Grid#____**

1. _____; U/P; Grid#____
2. _____; U/P; Grid#____
3. _____; U/P; Grid#____
4. _____; U/P; Grid#____
5. _____; U/P; Grid#____
6. _____; U/P; Grid#____
7. _____; U/P; Grid#____
8. _____; U/P; Grid#____
9. _____; U/P; Grid#____
10. _____; U/P; Grid#____

1. _____; U/P; Grid#____
2. _____; U/P; Grid#____
3. _____; U/P; Grid#____
4. _____; U/P; Grid#____
5. _____; U/P; Grid#____
6. _____; U/P; Grid#____
7. _____; U/P; Grid#____
8. _____; U/P; Grid#____
9. _____; U/P; Grid#____
10. _____; U/P; Grid#____

1. _____; U/P; Grid#____
2. _____; U/P; Grid#____
3. _____; U/P; Grid#____
4. _____; U/P; Grid#____
5. _____; U/P; Grid#____
6. _____; U/P; Grid#____
7. _____; U/P; Grid#____
8. _____; U/P; Grid#____
9. _____; U/P; Grid#____
10. _____; U/P; Grid#____

At the review interval that you select, e.g. daily, weekly, or monthly, *go back to the tasks that you accomplished and determine* 1) whether or not the things that you did were mostly planned or unplanned 2) if your tasks came from your Goal Tree assessment or from another source 3) if you were working on the things that mattered to you 4) if you were happy with your progress 5) what changes, if any, were needed.

At a future time, this tool will be coupled with our Goal Gauge to simplify making inputs to one's to do list. And, it will also be used to assist in personal goal forecasting and forensic evaluation of goal accomplishment(s) or failure(s).

"I Could Do Anything If Only I Knew What It Was"
Author : Barbara Sher

Musing RE: Distilled Goal Completion Quotient

Is a goal imbued with more power or meaning if it transits the Goal Discovery and Distillation Process? If so, how can we harness that power to use in our goal completion or goal renewal / expansion / enrichment? Is a goal that has been stripped of the elements, which would make it a pseudo-goal or an unspoken goal more likely to be accomplished? What process or tool(s) could enhance or enrich distilled goals even more?

Chapter 5 – A Model for success

- Success - Definitions
- Cognitive Dissonance
- Success Models - Individual Model
- Success Models - Team / Group Model
- Déjà vu – Success Revisited

- Expertise Matrix
- Designing An Expertise Matrix

Success – Definitions

It was very rare that I witnessed two workshop participants who had a similar definition of success. Thus, I will not try to define what success should mean to you - with the very limited exception of what successful personal planning and goal-setting should look like.

The two quotes that follow were introduced to workshop attendees due to their straight-forward meaning. The first definition suggests an unspoken adage, i.e. be careful of what you ask for, because you just might get it.

Success = Getting What You Want and Wanting What You Get

Source: Spokane Spokesman Review

**Successful People Form the Habit of Doing Things
That Failures Don't Like to Do.**

Source: Albert E.N. Gray's "The Common Denominator of Success"

This second quote, typically, led to discussions on habits. I would ask participants what were the most important habits for individuals to form. Some of the answers were: smiling, be prompt, say please and thank you, don't give up, and many more.

We wouldn't disparage any response. However, I would always add that I thought the most important habit to form was the habit of keeping promises to oneself. Part of the reason for this answer is that the populations which I served often had a "history" or track record of breaking promises to themselves.

Cognitive Dissonance

When one holds two conflicting thoughts or ideas in her mind at one time, she can be said to be experiencing dissonance. For example, if one believes that attaining success is a good thing, but at the same time, one realizes that success entails change. And, when one's experience with change has, heretofore, been unpleasant or bad, the following syllogism might illustrate the thinking and feeling one might experience:

Success=Good
Success=Change
Change=Bad
Success=Bad

When someone has discovered her goals and created plans to reach them, but fails to make progress towards those goals, cognitive dissonance might be playing – in the background – sabotaging her success at achieving or attaining her goal(s).

A stereotype of politicians is that she or he waffles or changes positions to suit the audience or issue. Imagine yourself at a political rally or town hall meeting. The politician is greeted with a great deal of concern over heightened crime in her district. She promises the crowd that she will author a bill or get funding for one or more new prisons. Back in Washington, D.C., her staff computes the needed taxes to build the prisons. She then places her newsletter on her web site with the new tax bill information. She, immediately, gets an earful from angry constituents opposing the new taxes. Thus, the syllogism goes:

Prisons=Good
Prisons=Taxes
Taxes=Bad
Prisons=Bad

Is it any wonder that we see politicians in such negative light? We send them our mixed messages on what we think we want or need sometimes, sans critical thinking.

Success Models – Individual Models

Guidelines:

We will be drawing word pictures of the individuals who embody success according to your definition of success. Who do you consider to be successful and why do you think that? We will examine the things that these individuals say/write; activities that you observe or read about that involve that successful role model. We will then list the things that you have observed about her or his appearance/ presence/ body language.

SUCCESSFUL ROLE MODEL(S):

A._____

B._____

C._____

WORDS - spoken or written:

1. _____
2. _____
3. _____
4. _____
5. _____

ACTIONS:

1. _____
2. _____
3. _____
4. _____
5. _____

APPEARANCE:

1. _____
2. _____
3. _____
4. _____
5. _____

Success Models – Team/Group Models

Let's turn our attention to what elements make up a successful team. Feel free to use a successful team that you have belonged to or one that you are a fan of. Please select at least three different teams work teams, sports teams or marriages / families, if you are so inclined.

SUCCESSFUL TEAM MODEL(S):

A._____

B._____

C._____

WORDS:

1. _____
2. _____
3. _____
4. _____
5. _____

DEEDS:

1. _____
2. _____
3. _____
4. _____
5. _____

APPEARANCE:

1. _____
2. _____
3. _____
4. _____
5. _____

The information gleaned from the individual success model combined with the team success model can inform an individual or a team of the elements which yield or sustain a successful environment for each.

As an individual, we can model the speech, actions, and appearance (how the successful role model presents herself to the public not mimicking her presentation or wardrobe, per se). And for a team, we can pull together team members which embody the elements of/ from the successful team.

We can create success from the success of others. Put another way, motivational speaker, Tony Robbins says that success leaves clues - that statement is true of an individual or of a team. We can incorporate these clues into a successful individual or team persona(s) for ourselves and the teams and groups that we are a part of.

Revisiting Success

I have had the pleasure of conducting scores of workshops for participants from populations we label welfare-to-work, ex-offenders, displaced homemakers, long-term underemployed, at-risk youth, etc. These workshops covered life skills, job search, motivation, self-esteem, etc.

In these workshops, many participants found it difficult to recall or believe that they have had any successes. Hence, the following exercises wherein we looked at recent and not-so-recent successes distilling the emotions that prevailed when we attained the listed success.

Please take the time to list at least 3 accomplishments in the last 12 months, then list 3 in the last 5 years, and lastly list 3 from more than 10 years ago.

"DEJA VU" - Success Revisited

Accomplishment(s):

Emotion(s):

Last 12 mos.

(a)_____

Emotion:_____

(b)_____

Emotion:_____

(c)_____

Emotion:_____

Last 5 years:

(a)_____

Emotion:_____

(b)_____

Emotion:_____

(c)_____

Emotion:_____

10+ yrs. Ago

(a)_____

Emotion:_____

(b)_____

Emotion:_____

(c)_____

Emotion:_____

It is very likely that you will come up with more than three accomplishments for each of the prescribed time periods. If so, freely list any additional accomplishment(s) to these lists.

Our next step, once we capture the positive emotions attendant to our previous accomplishments, is to plan or forecast accomplishments over the near term along with the long term - incorporating the positive emotions that we have listed.

Future Accomplishments:

Next 24 mos.:

(a)_____

Emotion:_____

(b) _____

Emotion:_____

(c) _____

Emotion:_____

Next 2-5 yrs.

(a) _____

Emotion:_____

(b) _____

Emotion:_____

(c) _____

Emotion:_____

The Expertise Matrix

The Expertise Matrix gives you a snapshot of the skills and knowledge that you are able to offer the job market or your current employer at a given point in time. The Expertise Matrix also has the flexibility to give you a snapshot of what your skill set looked like at a point in the past, e.g. 5 or 10 years ago.

You can also project into the future what your skills and knowledge will look like at a given point in time, e.g. after a degree completion or after an apprenticeship program.

The Expertise Matrix can also be used by a team or group to capture the skills and knowledge available or planned, e.g. pre or post merger or acquisition. It is only limited by your imagination.

The following example is one that I prepared for myself 2-3 years ago to illustrate the skills and knowledge that I could offer a prospective client, a customer, or a reader once my product(s) was developed or published.

Expertise Matrix Example

Expertise Matrix

	CLIENT	Grades 9-12	Higher Ed	Individuals	Teams	Organizations
PRODUCT						
Activity Mgmt System [1]		X^{BC}	X^{ISC}	X^{BIS}	X^{IS}	X^{IS}
FMBOK + CoP [2]		X^{B}	X^{BCS}	X^{BDS}	X^{BS}	X^{BIS}
Indiv Strat Plng & GDDP [3]		X^{BCI}	X^{BCDI}	X^{BDIS}		
Vision Mapping [4]		X^{B}	X^{BCI}	X^{BDIS}	X^{BIS}	X^{BIS}
Problem-Solving & DM [5]		Y	Y	Y		
Orgn'l Strat Mgmt & VMA w/Job Desc [6]						Y^{IS}
Job Search Workshop [7]		Y^{BCI}	X^{BCI}	X^{BDIS}		X^{BIS}
TEEN & SEEN [8]		X^{BI}	X^{BCI}			Y^{BI}
Customized Services		Y	Y	Y	Y	Y

LEGEND –
1. Activity Management System
2. Failure Mngmt Book of Knowledge & Community of Practice
3. Indiv Strategic Plng + Goal Discovery & Distillation Process;
4. Vision M.A.P.
5. Problem-Solving & Decision Making
6. Organizational Strategic Management & Vision-Mission Alignment w/Job Descriptions
7. Job Search Workshops
8. Teen Employment & Entrepreneurial Network and Student Employment & Entrepreneurial Network
9. Customized Services

LEGEND FOR - "X" - The Delivery Method, i.e. B=Book; C=Course; D=Disk; I=Internet; S=Seminar

" " "Y" – Prospective or Planned Delivery Methods

"The genesis of wasted time is in time spent on unwritten goals"

Designing an Expertise Matrix

My Expertise Matrix, above, is comprised of training programs that I have developed [**what**], the intended audiences for the training [**who**], and the delivery method(s) I could use [**how**].

In developing your Expertise Matrix, ask yourself **what** skills and knowledge (skills set) do I have; **where** can I employ my skills set; **who** are the end users for my skills set; **how much** are people currently paying for my skills set; **when** can I begin delivering my skills set to prospective employers or clients; **why** would / do people pay for my skills set?

The Expertise Matrix can be used to capture past skills and knowledge or future skills and knowledge. The Expertise Matrix gives you a snapshot of your skills and knowledge – past, present or future.

Be the Expert, as stated in chapter one,

You Are The World's Foremost Expert
And Authority On Your Dreams,
Loves, Desires, and Likes

As well as Your Shoulds, Musts,
Have Tos, and Dislikes

By capturing and distilling success clues from others, individuals, and teams, we can create goals for ourselves, on an on-going basis as we complete, i.e. obtain and/or attain those goals.

With the tools in this and the next chapter we establish success and then work towards becoming congruent with that definition of success. Again, be the expert you don't have to become the expert or become the authority on your needs and wants you already are the world's foremost expert and authority on you.

Musing RE: Goal(s) Reciprocity Quotient

One's priorities or goals can be subsumed in/by one's work or mate or family. We, can, effectively, lose our identity or goal priorities to others. The Goal(s) Reciprocity Quotient would tell us, in advance, if we are at risk of having our goals relegated to an inferior position in relation to other's goal, i.e. work, mate, or family.

Perhaps, there are times that it is okay to voluntarily place our goals on hold in deference to another individual or to a cause or for an employer. But, this should be a conscious decision that you enter into, willingly.

Chapter 6 - Building and Maintaining a Success Inventory

- The Success Inventory
- Resources - Internal and External
- Barriers - Internal and External
- Personal Employment Planning Profile
  - Market Profile
  - Value Creation Profile
  - Competencies Profile
  - Resource Use Profile
- Networking

The Success Inventory

This chapter focuses on increasing our awareness of and access to the abundant resources, which await our request or demand. The following tools will help you to assess typical resources and possible barriers to your success.

Whether you are using this workbook for your own benefit or you are helping someone else achieve her goals, this workbook will outline and detail thought-provoking and action-oriented activities which will result in an individual strategic plan for you or her.

Assessing Our Resources and Barriers to Success

The following lists are not intended to be all inclusive. These lists should serve as a springboard to your examination of the people and things which can assist you in the accomplishment of your dreams and desires.

Feel free to more or fewer categories to the ones, below. If you are examining people as resources, one can look at a specific family member / co- worker for help in one area and another family member or co-worker for help in another area. You may find counselors or clergy, also. Please do not be limited by the written word.

GOAL RESOURCES

People:

Family: Specify_____

Friends: Specify_____

Professionals: Specify_____

Work/Business: Specify_____

Educational: Specify_____

Government: Specify_____

Financial:

Net Worth: Specify_____

Personal: Specify_____

Credit Score: Specify_____

Network: Specify_____

Corporate: Specify_____

Things:

Data: Specify_____

Tools: Specify_____

Natural

Resources: Specify_____

Other: Specify_____

Internal:

Vision: Specify_____

Faith: Specify_____

LOVE: Specify_____

Enthusiasm: Specify_____

Knowledge: Specify_____

Persistence: Specify_____

Resilience: Specify_____

Other: Specify_____

GOAL BARRIERS

Internal:

Beliefs: Specify_____

Reputation: Specify_____

Finances: Specify_____

Education: Specify_____

Looks: Specify_____

Age: Specify_____

Health: Specify_____

Other: Specify_____

External:

People: Specify_____

Institutions: Specify_____

Family: Specify_____

Credit: Specify_____

Fate/Luck: Specify_____

Ethnicity: Specify_____

Gender: Specify_____

Other: Specify_____

S.Y.I.

See yourself into new situations:

Safely
Happily
Easily

I have seen participants transfer or generalize a failure, such as the loss of a job, loss of a loved one, divorce, dropping out of school into a lifelong deprecation of their personal efficacy. By the same token, you can transfer or generalize success(es) to any situation that you find yourself in - beginning and maintaing a new lifelong appreciation of your personal efficacy or ability to make things happen. The exercises in this chapter will serve as a reminder or alarm clock for those who have forgotten or not considered themselves as having efficacy or personal power.

Personal Employment Planning Profile

Employment or work plays (or played) an important part of most of our lives. Finding work entails a variety of skills and self-knowledge as well as knowledge of the labor market.

One of my favorite volumes from grad school was Strategic Management by Drs. Charles Hill and Gareth Jones, published by Houghton Mifflin, 2001. This rather large volume was dedicated to the strategic management of organizations. But, an un-explored application of this otherwise excellent work is its application to you and I in terms of a search for employment.

For the sake of our discussion, I will call this new application the personal employment planning profile. This matrix consists of four quadrants or parts, they are:

1. **Market Profile**
2. **Value Creation Profile**
3. **Competencies Profile**
4. **Resource Use Profile**

The organization which you wish to join has a posture or profile in terms of its interface with its markets, e.g. low price strategy, differentiation strategy, focus strategy, or a blend of the foregoing orientations.

Where does your education and experience place you in terms of helping your prospective employer meet its marketplace goals? Is your present or last employer using one or more of these strategies to gain or maintain market share? If you don't know - find out!

Value Creation is what your prospective employer must add to the products or services it provides. Does this prospective employer work with / on the inputs, processes, or the outputs or a combination of the foregoing? What skills and knowledge do you have that can enhance the work performed by your new employer?

Just as individuals have competencies so, too, do organizations. The four major competencies are:

1. **Efficiency**
2. **Quality**
3. **Innovation**
4. **Customer Responsiveness**

Organizations use these competencies to attract and keep customers. Again, you can assess your education and experience to help your next employer increase its market share.

The proper focus on these elements of strategic management allows for an organization's continued(ing) viability. Resources include (in this order) people, money, and/or data and tools. How many and how well have you led / managed others; what size budgets have you managed;

do you have security clearances, do you have expertise in information technology, what type of tools do you employ on a regular basis?

Networking

Networking oftentimes involves a center of influence a person or people who can refer, recommend, or suggest a contact person for something of value that the recipient of this referral seeks. For example, if I am looking for a position in a given field, my center of influence may recommend that I contact someone she knows who has an opportunity or information that would be helpful to me in my search. That referral could be a hiring manager, an industry source for training, or a head hunter.

The form, below, helps you to keep track of referrals from your center(s) of influence. With this form, you can log and track progress on each referral as well as keep your center of influence informed. To make your network effective, treat your center of influence and all referrals with the utmost respect. And, show **gratitude** towards your center of influence for all leads and information that you receive - make it your practice to send a thank you card (message) to each referral that assists you. You can also help others with these rudiments of networking so that person can also obtain positive results from her networking.

Networking Form

INDIVIDUAL STRATEGIC PLANNING
NETWORK

Center(s) of Influence: Name: _____ Title:_____ Company:_____
Address:_____ Phone:_____

☐ Relative ☐ Friend ☐ Co-worker ☐ Customer/Client ☐ Professional Assn. ☐ Union ☐ School   ☐ Military ☐
Employment Agency ☐ Government Agency ☐ Other_____

REFERRALS

1. Name:_____ Title:_____ Company:_____
Address:_____ Phone/FAX:_____
*How was this contact made?_____ Date of Contact:_____
Date for Thank You Note:_____ **Result of Contact: _____
Follow-up (+ dates for each contact): _____
_____
_____

2. Name:_____Title:_____Company:_____
Address:_____Phone/FAX:_____
How was this contact made?_____ Date of Contact:_____
Date for Thank You note:_____ Result of Contact:_____
Follow-up (+dates for each contact): _____
_____
_____

3. Name:_____ Title:_____ Company:_____
Address:_____Phone/FAX:_____
How was this contact made?_____ Date of Contact:_____
Date for Thank You note:_____ Result of Contact:_____
Follow-up (+dates for each contact): _____
_____
_____

*How was this contact made---That is Phone Call, Letter, Meeting or introduction from a mutual friend or acquaintance.

**Such as New Referral, Helpful Information, Job Lead, Job Offer, Training Opportunity, Information Interview , No Contact, Not Helpful, Other...

NOTE: Keep your Center of Influence informed on your progress! And be sure to thank her or him for any referrals or job leads!

Musing RE: Resource(s) vs Barrier(s) Over Time

Over time is it more likely that resources will increase as barriers decrease? Or is the opposite true? What role do experience and confidence play in garnering resources to overcome barriers, if any?

Is there a ratio or relationship of resources to barriers? Does it increase with education? Does it increase with time? Is this ratio or relationship the same or similar amongst people of the same age group (e.g. 20-29 or 30-39)?

What other factors increase the ratio of resources to barriers? Is it better to increase resources or to decrease barriers?

Chapter 7 - Metrics

- Metrics
- Clues - Success
- Critical Success Factors List
- Clues - Failure
- Critical Failure Factors List
- Point Schedule
- Point Schedule Summary
- Prosperity Calendar
- Next Use of Funds
- Entry Strategies List
- Exit Strategies List
- De-briefing Strategy

METRICS

Motivational speaker and personal development guru, Tony Robbins, says that "Success Leaves Clues" - clues to the traits and behaviors necessary to replicate the success that is being modeled. Drs. Stanton and George of Saint Joseph's University state that "failure leaves clues" in their book, *Success Leaves Clues*.

Metrics are established to keep score. However, one has to name the game so to speak to give the metrics meaning. For example, if one undertakes a job search (the why for the activity), how does one know that she is on the right track towards employment? What should she be doing?

How much activity should she be engaged in? These are the meta-metrics in this case, the precursors of the actual metrics contained in the job search tool, below, i.e. The Point Schedule used by thousands of workshop attendees and web site visitors.

There is enough information in all of our lives to construct or re-construct the successes that we seek. Our awareness of the success of others gives us the clues as to the elements which need to be incorporated into our lives to give us the measure of success that we seek.

Clues – Success

This list of Critical Success Factors contains elements and activities which are associated with successful outcomes. It is far from being complete, but it will be a springboard to the individual or team that wants to ensure a greater likelihood of success. If we do or possess the following, we increase our chances for success:

1. Written Action or Project Plan
2. Dry Run/Rehearsal both processes and desired results
3. Engage in Scenario Planning
4. Knowledge - Tacit and Explicit
5. Identify one's Network and use it
6. Community of Practice – join or establish
7. Metrics - quantify results for measurement purposes
8. Identify resources, i.e. people, financial info, data, and tools needed
9. Resiliency - bounce back from set-backs
10. Remain motivated to continually work on your plan
11. Love those you serve as well as those that rely on you
12. Risk Management Plan - assess and plan around and through obstacles
13. Communication Plan - Distilling feedback / data to inform stakeholders of plan fulfillment
14. Vision and Mission - Provide the motivation and direction for effort
15. Decision Support System scientific support systems for forecasting and forensics

The Pacific Institute of Seattle, WA teaches its clients about the Reticular Activating System (RAS) this netlike sheath of cells covers a portion of the brain. The purpose of the RAS is to alert one to opportunities or to danger. For example, if you were invited to participate in a scavenger hunt and could win $100,000 for each of the following prizes if you could gather all the items in the next eight hours - how many could you come up with?

1. A photo of a soldier in uniform
2. A photo of a blue house
3. A Rubik's cube
4. A floppy disk
5. A cassette tape

If this were a genuine contest and the prizes had value for you, your mind would work overtime, if necessary, to alert you to every opportunity to get paid for the fulfillment of the five items, above. It is the RAS that keeps the image of the needed items at the top of mind in terms of awareness.

When new parents bring their child home for the first time, one or both of them are on guard to check on the child at any time. The RAS alerts the parent to movement or sounds that the child makes. Another example is a person can hear their name called above the din of an outdoor sporting event or in a crowded auditorium - that is the RAS at work.

One can also be on guard in terms of being aware of the Critical Failure Factors or CFFs (or CSFs), which could be a part of the work one is engaged in or in a relationship that one values.

Clues – Failure

Critical Failure Factors are attributes or conditions which make failure more likely to occur. My first list of CFFs had about eighty entries. It was pared down to reduce duplication and confusion from similar sounding factors.

Each failure that one experiences could be the result of a combination of CFFs or just one CFF. There is no known way [to this author] to anticipate which CFFs will plague a given project. However, an understanding of common CFFs may make the individual more aware or cautious if a given CFF becomes apparent.

The CFFs that follow are a small sampling of the myriad possible CFFs.

1. Character flaws
2. Conditioning - negative
3. Discipline - lack of
4. Knowledge - lack of
5. Resources - not enough of the right things
6. Thinking and Reasoning - failure to apply
7. Vision - no
8. Metrics - undefined or poorly defined
9. Conflict - personality or dissonance
10. Sabotage - self or by another (others)
11. Motivation - apathetic towards an end result
12. Communication - lack of or poor
13. Leadership - selfish and/or myopic
14. Culture - lack of knowledge of
15. Work Ethic - anemic or non-existent
16. Expectations - not communicated
17. Deception - deliberate mis-direction
18. Error/Falsity - may be inadvertent

Again, each of our lives is replete with success clues and failure clues. And, once we learn how to navigate around and through the waters containing these clues, we will begin to experience success upon success.

Next, we explore a tool, which had its origins in U.S. Census Bureau data (1980-2000). The Point Schedule is an example of a tool that has forecasting potential in terms of helping one find a job. The use of metrics assists us in metering our activity while engaging in the critical success factors for finding a job.

POINT SCHEDULE

Guidelines:

The primary assumption behind this tool - based on 15 years experience using it - is that The Point Schedule helps the end user engage in the activities that lead to landing a job – according to Census Bureau data.

When I developed this tool, the level of activity it entailed exceeded that required by our state's Employment Security Department for job finding success. It keeps the job seeker busy with result-oriented activities. Each of the listed activities has a point total associated with it. And, each day the job seeker completes a preset point total in furtherance of her job search.

POINT SCHEDULE

Points ----- Activities

1 point 1. Search want ads of newspaper or professional journal

2 pts.   2. Visit the Job Service Center to review computer listings

2 pts.   3. Complete an online application

2 pts.   4. Blind leads---Mail resumes to "prospective employers"

2 pts. 5. Visit libraries---Ask reference librarian about job info

3 pts. 6. Mail resume and cover letter in response to ad

3 pts. 7. Contact employment agency (in person)

4 pts. 8. Visit personnel offices to check job boards

4 pts. 9. Talk to employed people (whether you are acquainted with them

or not) and inquire about jobs at their companies

5 pts. 10. Visit employer to pick up application

5 pts. 11. Visit employer to fill out an application

8 pts. 12. Initial interview*

10 pts. 13. Follow-up interview*

10 pts. 14. Job search training workshops (2+ hours/day)

10 pts. 15. Job Offer

***If you are late to an interview, subtract 3 points**

NOTE: You must obtain 15 points per day (M-F) using this method

Completed point schedule activities can be compiled using the Point Schedule Summary. This form allows one to keep track of the day-to-day activities she engages in as part of her job hunt.

#					PERSONAL STRATEGIC PLANNING		
					POINT SCHEDULE SUMMARY		
	DATE:	POINTS	COMPANY	NAME OF CONTACT	PHONE #	JOB WANTED	ACTIVITY/ COMMENTS
1							
2							
3							
4							
5							
6							
7							
8							
9							
10							
11							
12							
13							
14							
15							
16							
17							
18							
19							
20							
21							
22							
23							
24							
25							
26							
27							
28							
29							
30							

THE PROSPERITY CALENDAR

Envision "Increased" Prosperity

The information comprising The Prosperity Calendar has previously been formatted into something that was nothing more than a debt calendar that informed you of how long you would be in debt.

The difference here is that The Prosperity Calendar now tells an individual when her financial windfalls or opportunities are scheduled. Coupled with the Next Use of Funds form, an individual, couple, or group can plan the future use of her or their money.

												PERSONAL STRATEGIC PLANNING							
												Prosperity Calendar							
			MONTHS OF THE FIRST YEAR												YEARS 2-7				COMMENTS
CREDITOR	BALANCE	PAYMENT	1st	2nd	3rd	4th	5th	6th	7th	8th	9th	10th	11th	12th	Yr.2	Yr.3	Yr.4	Yr.5	Yr.6	Yr.7	PIF=PAID IN FULL
1	$	$																		
2	$	$																		
3	$	$																		
4	$	$																		
5	$	$																		
6	$	$																		
7	$	$																		
8	$	$																		
9	$	$																		
10	$	$																		
11	$	$																		
12	$	$																		
13	$	$																		
14	$	$																		
15	$	$																		
16	$	$																		
17	$	$																		
18	$	$																		
19	$	$																		
20	$	$																		

Guidelines:

The [Next] Use of Funds Statement is self-explanatory as to the information required to complete it. The purpose is to have you commit to (put in writing) a plan for personal financial success. Typically, debts evidence an installment contract for monthly or periodic payments. When these payments end, you are entitled to re-allocate these funds in any way that you choose – choose options wherein your funds appreciate in value, first.

INDIVIDUAL STRATEGIC PLANNING
[NEXT] USE OF FUNDS STATEMENT

Current Creditor:_____
Purpose of Debt:_____
Amount Owed: $_____
Monthly Installment: $_____
Date Debt Will Be Paid-In-Full_____

1. **NEXT USE FOR THESE FUNDS** (Monthly Installment):_____
_____.

2. Amount *RESERVED/COMMITTED* for Investment, "Permanent" Savings or
retirement: $_____ (50% of monthly installment amount-recommended)

3. Date new *USE FOR FUNDS* is to begin:_____

4. LENGTH OF COMMITMENT to this new program:_____ (a period
equal to the "installment term" this new program replaced **is recommended**)

5. *DEFAULT* on this new "contract" shall mean: _____
_____
_____.

6. *REMEDY* for default shall be limited to: _____
_____
_____.

7. Emergency Provision (*HARDSHIP*): _____
_____
_____.

(Access to the funds under this new "contract" shall be limited to the above listed
circumstances)

Signature:_____   Signature:_____

[OPTIONAL]

Witness:_____   Witness:_____

NOTARY:_____

In creating an individual strategic plan, we find that our plan includes the acquisition of things, e.g. house, car, boat, rv, etc., we must realize that many of these things, typically, result in debt. Recall the information on cognitive dissonance, above. Let's create a new syllogism regarding our goals to acquire things or to do certain things, i.e:

Goals=good
Goals=spending
Spending=debt
Debt=bad

Goals=bad???

Here we are not judging one's thinking or feeling as being good or bad. And, spending does not always entail debt - so there is no need for guilt or fear. If you are now experiencing uncertainty or vacillation about your goal choices, it may be due to the, aforementioned, dissonance.

Material Desires = Price Tag = *Unspoken Debt!*

Entry Strategies

Most people can insinuate themselves into activities or groups that they want to be a part of. A question that arises is - was there a more optimal entry strategy than the one that she chose?

Youth will benefit from the knowledge of entry strategies by learning how to initiate associations with healthy groups and activities. And former youth may enhance their current circle of friends and groups they belong to.

Please take a moment to construct a list of options for joining a group, company, volunteer activity, etc. that you want to be a part of. Examples of the means/methods for joining the group or activity, include:

1. Academic and/or Technical Preparation
2. Accident
3. Audition
4. Barter
5. Buy-in (financial)
6. Daydream/Fantasize
7. Favor
8. Force
9. Mentored
10. On-the-job training
11. Proposal: Written, Oral or Multi-media
12. Self-taught

13. Nomination
14. Referral
15. Recommendation
16. Pass a test
17. Court order

Exit Strategies

A good plan contains an exit strategy. There usually are a number of options for extrication if planned for in advance - preferably along with the planned entry strategy. Many people find themselves trapped in associations and relationships that are not conducive to their well-being. An exit strategy can help the user to map the way out of the association, relationship, or activity - safely, happily, and easily in advance of aligning with or joining the group or activity. Exit Strategies are best formulated before one joins a group or activity. However, if we did not plan, in advance, consider:

1. resigning with or without notice
2. paying a fee
3. signing an agreement
4. going to court
5. obtaining counseling services
6. consulting someone who has extricated herself from this or a similar situation, etc.

Exit Strategies are often developed for dis-engaging from the following types of obligations:

1. Business
2. Crime/Abuse
3. Education
4. Employment
5. Habits
6. Investments
7. Legal/Contracts
8. Relationships/Roles
9. Routines
10. Volunteer Activities

Debriefing Strategy

Whether or not one's plan is successful, one needs to learn from it. Successful strategies and tactics become a part of one's (tacit or explicit) knowledge base for use, personally or interpersonally. And, if one is not successful, that failure represents an opportunity to learn the lessons of that endeavor and become better prepared the next time.

The de-brief covers both the efficacy of the entry strategy as well as the exit strategy along with the actual results obtained. The middle portion, i.e. operation or processes are reviewed as well. Although, one person can recount the entry and exit strategies, alone, de-briefing takes two or more people to work best. Developing a scenario(s) for what would / should happen if a situation was to recur is also a helpful exercise.

Musing RE: _**Success and Failure Insertion Points**_

My experience and education have afforded me the opportunity to observe people and businesses. One of those observations can be stated in this way:

Processes and activities are subject to the advent of one or more critical success factors or critical failure factors (listed herein). Our awareness of these factors prepares us for the possible (conscious or unconscious) introduction of CSFs or CFFs into a process or activity, thereby seeding that activity with the hypothetical "success germ" or "failure germ".

An illustration of this phenomenon is found in the adage about turning lemons into lemonade. This adage suggests that that there is an intervention(s), which can seed a negative situation and turn it into a positive situation. Another example is the phrase, she pulled failure out of the jaws of success - the converse of the lemonade illustration.

This musing stems from numerous personal observations. The notion that there are success and failure insertion points should be researched, formally, as the benefits of knowing what to do and when to do it in a process or activity to ensure success are incalculable.

Chapter 8 - The Wrap-up

- My Individual Strategic Plan Package - Final Product
- Updating My Plan
- The Follow-up Schedule
- What's My Motivation?

"Final Product" Checklist

Your Individual Strategic Plan Package includes the following elements, below. The purpose of this step is to bring each of the components together into one spot (a manila folder is adequate, initially). There is no requirement to review each component at each of your chosen intervals. For example, Deja Vu or re-visiting success over the past 1-10 years is not necessary for a weekly, monthly, or maybe even a quarterly review. However, one's "Linked To Do Lists" would benefit from a daily or weekly review, but the choice is yours in terms of which components require a more frequent review.

THE **SELF-IMAGE GRID** completed. Please use the **BLANK** Self-Image Grid - adding roles and characteristics meaningful to you. _____

THE **TEAM-IMAGE GRID** presents a "snapshot" of your team in terms of behavior and characteristics...teams to form/join, also. _____

THE SUCCESS MODEL. A list of: A) Words B) Actions C) Appearance from a successful role model(s) and a successful team model(s), also. _____

DEJA VU - Re-visiting your successes - from the earliest to the latest. _____

Discover a full-range of prospective goals from **THE GOAL TREE** exercise. _____

Goal balance with/from **THE GOAL GRID** _____

THE INVENTORY of Resources and Barriers for goal realization. _____

Financial "Clarity" with **THE PROSPERITY CALENDAR**. _____

NEXT USE OF FUNDS - Answers: Who, What, When, Where, Why, How Much and What to do next with your money? _____

Planning/Feedback System put into place. Feedback on each day's activities w/**THE LINKED TO DO LIST** _____

Coordinate "relationship" goals with **THE GOAL CIRCLES** _____

THE POINT SCHEDULE - if needed _____

THE FOLLOW-UP schedule determine what activities are necessary for your current situation and the interval for each. _____

THE GOAL GLOSSARY - This set of definitions is included because there really is a goal-setting "lingo". This glossary will help you to learn that language of goal-setting in a fun way – tying these concepts together. _____

Guidelines:

Much of the value of individual strategic planning is realized over time. And, the way to maintain one's course is to re-visit the plan often and make adjustment if/when required.

Initially, it is better to make more frequent follow-ups to ensure the realization of your plan(s). As time goes by, one may be able to use less frequent intervals for updates.

The Follow-up Schedule

The following guideline provides a tentative review schedule that you may wish to follow. Re-visiting these worksheets at regular intervals provides you with the opportunity to make needed or desired changes in furtherance of your goal discovery and goal distillation efforts. These are only suggestions as you may find a schedule that works better for you.

Daily or Weekly Review

The Linked To Do List

The Point Schedule (if applicable)

Monthly Review

The Linked To Do List

The Goal Grid

Goal Circles

Resources & Barriers

Success Model

The Point Schedule (if applicable)

Quarterly Review

The Linked To Do List

The Prosperity Calendar

Self-Image Grid

Team-Image Grid

School-Image Grid (if applicable)

The Goal Grid

Goal Circles

Resources & Barriers

Success Model

The Point Schedule (if applicable)

Annual Review – All Relevant Documents

The Linked To Do List

The Prosperity Calendar

Self-Image Grid

Team-Image Grid

School-Image Grid (if applicable)

The Goal Grid

Goal Circles

Resources & Barriers

Success Model

The Goal Tree

The Follow-up Schedule

MOTIVATION

Motivation is one of those terms that is, frequently, misunderstood. Therefore, I will define it as follows:

Motivation is a contraction of the words, motive and action. Motive is typically understood to mean a reason or purpose. Action is typically understood to mean motion or behavior. Thus, motivation is moving in the direction of a reason or purpose.

My next question is what are people motivated to do. What I have learned is that people are motivated to 1) gain a benefit 2) avoid a negative situation. Number two is derived from number one as it allows an individual the opportunity to maintain the status quo. I believe that everyone is motivated, i.e. motivated to gain a benefit.

Musing RE: *Employer vs. Employee Locus for Expertise Development*

Whose responsibility is expertise development - the employer or employee? What are the benefits and drawbacks of fostering an employer oriented program of resource development? And, what are the benefits and drawbacks of having an employee-oriented resource development program? Are these interests complementary or are these interests in conflict?

Chapter 9 - Special Preview

- The Idea Realization Continuum
- The Vision Continuum and Vision MAP
- Strategic Alignment of Your Job Description w/Your Organization's Vision and Mission
- Risk Management
- Failure Management
- Employee Footprint

Idea Realization Continuum

The idea realization continuum proposes the notion that ideas have a track to run on to completion. And, that the track is knowable and subject to conscious planning and forensic investigation. Our idea realization continuum will be called the **Vision Continuum -** this Vision Continuum features a seven step process from ideation to end result or desired outcome.

The components of the Vision Continuum were defined in chapter 3, above. Briefly, the components - in order, are:

1. Vision(s)
2. Mission(s)
3. Plan(s)
4. Goal(s)
5. Objective(s)
6. Task(s)
7. End Result(s) or Desired Outcome(s)

Our Vision Continuum is displayed as a slice of pie. That pie is then aggregated into a whole pie based on related components. For example, if we are discussing an individual, we list elements that may be germane to the person's life, e.g.

- **Career**
- **Community**
- **Education**
- **Family**
- **Health - Mental**
- **Health - Physical**
- **Personal**

- **Relationship**
- **Social**
- **Spiritual**

You will, probably, recall that these elements were part of the Goal Grid and the goal distillation process in chapter 4, above. The aggregated slices of pie are displayed in what we call a Vision MAP. This Vision MAP is a snapshot of the current state of the user's life in terms of the elements she chose to incorporate into the Vision MAP.

Teams or groups can produce one or more Vision MAPs for the team or group and their respective members. Organizations of any size can use Vision MAPs to illustrate the current state, future state (forecast), or past state (forensic) offering snapshots of the desired time period(s).

A married couple can use a Vision MAP to better align the individual, the marriage, and the family. An organization can align a team with a department or division along with an entire organization. The permutations are endless.

Within this system of Vision MAPs, there is a Vision Breakdown Structure (VBS), which allows one to display components of the Vision MAP in such a way that each can be analyzed. The VBS allows us to reverse engineer results.

Each family member or each employee will have a vista of the family or organizations that will help her grasp a holistic perspective on that family or organization. And she will also be able to see areas for improvement as well as develop a means to see the changes all the way through to the desired outcome(s).

Strategic Alignment of Your Job Description w/Your Organization's Vision and Mission

One of my doctoral research projects entailed collecting available data to determine whether or not organizations' job / position descriptions were tethered to or aligned with the organizations' vision and mission statements.

The resounding answer was no. And, why is this fact significant, you ask. One wonders, why do the work, if there is not a direct link between an organization's vision and mission and the jobs that are filled to accomplish the work of the organization.

It should matter to the organization, because it would likely matter to the employee that there is a nexus between their work and the organization's vision and mission.

An organization's vision and mission should appear as figurative (if not actual) watermarks in each of its job / position descriptions.

Risk Management

The four areas of risk management as it pertains to the individual in individual strategic planning are:

a. Risk Quantification

b. Risk Mitigation

c. Reward Quantification

d. Reward Enhancement

These areas will be added to future editions, both online and in print.

Failure Management

Another research project entailed a foray into personal failure analysis and management – the subject of a new workbook. I read publications by thought leaders in the field of human failure analysis and management. And, then I wrote letters and emails to them.

My letter suggested that we form a community of practice to develop a body of knowledge on this and allied topics. The Critical Failure Factors were one of the areas researched during this project.

Employee Footprint

My introduction to the concept of an employee footprint left me with the impression that the term was only applicable to accounting and finance circles. Along these lines a company would look at the financial impact an employee has on its bottom line.

Another viewpoint entails seeing an employee's perspective in terms of her actual and potential impact on that same organization or any other organization. The latter point of view empowers the employee or applicant for a position. The former point of view portrays the employee as a burden, which must be accounted for – as the employee may be seen as a drag on profitability.

Musing RE: The efficacy of the system of Vision Mapping components

Taken, individually, a vision; a mission; a plan; a goal; an objective; a task; or an end result, do not need to be researched to establish the value of each term. But, as a Vision Continuum (or Vision MAPs) that research appears to be, in order.

Although, this information has been shared with workshop participants, there has been no formal research regarding its efficacy or transferability to other people or groups.

Perhaps, these musings will prompt more investigation into the efficacy of the tools and the processes that we call Vision Mapping.

ASSESSMENT (Back-end)

In the Preface to this workbook, I promised you that you would be able to do the following things upon the completion of this workbook. Let's try now to complete the assessment.

Although, this is technically a self-assessment, it is also an author-assessment in terms of how well did I do my job of explaining the "what to do" and "how to do" of succeeding at personal planning and goal setting.

1. List three activities that you desire most to do and three activities that you need most to do. Feel free to consult the goal-setting tools that you have developed.

a. Desire to do

i. _____

ii. _____

iii. _____

b. Need to do

i. _____

ii. _____

iii. _____

2. Set priorities based on desires and needs listed in #1.

a. Desire #1 _____

b. Desire #2 _____

c. Desire #3 _____

a. Need #1 _____

b. Need #2 _____

c. Need #3 _____

3. Set daily to do activities and priorities based on your needs and needs.

Describe how you have used this information in planning daily activities. If you have not used it, please explain why not.

_____

_____

_____

4. Name (and give examples of) at least four Activity Management Concepts.

a. _____

b. _____

c. _____

d. _____

5. Name 5 Critical Success Factors and 5 Critical Failure Factors in the individual strategic planning process.

a. Success factors

i._____

ii._____

iii._____

iv._____

v. _____

b. Failure factors

i._____

ii._____

iii._____

iv._____

v. _____

6. List at least three components of the Expertise Matrix.

a._____

b._____

c. _____

7. Create a follow-up schedule to keep your plan on track to completion.

Summarize what follow-up activities you will do and when you will do the activity.

_____

_____

_____

8. Name three success traits that you admire in others or seek to acquire

a. _____

b. _____

c. _____

9. List at least three entry and three exit strategies for attaining a goal that you seek.

a. Entry Strategy

i._____

ii._____

iii._____

b. Exit Strategy

i._____

ii._____

iii._____

Postscript

I have developed a healthy respect for all authors of all genres as I have labored over the contents and format and feel of this book for close to three years. The biggest struggle was in what to leave out as it is not easy to condense over 30 years of experience into 150 pages or so. However, the solution to that problem is remedied by writing subsequent books (and blog posts) and articles on related topics.

The self-help authors that I have read over the years provided me with an invaluable service by packaging their tacit knowledge into digestible morsels between the pages of the hundreds of books and articles that I read.

I trust that this workbook also provides you with tools to accomplish, attain, or acquire your heart's desires and that you will likewise share your collective knowledge with others that are becoming.

Regardless of which goal setting system you espouse, the following advice is priceless!

Press On

Nothing in the world can take the place of persistence,
Talent will not; nothing is more common
than unsuccessful men with talent,
Genius will not; unrewarded genius is
almost a proverb,
Education will not; the world is full of educated derelicts.
Persistence and determination alone are omnipotent.
The slogan *Press On* has solved and always will solve
the problems of the human race.

By J. Calvin Coolidge
30th President of the United States of America

APPENDIX A

Generally speaking, these "old forms" are useful to show how some of the information for the Goal Discovery and Distillation Process was displayed. But, it also serves as a springboard for you to use to format these data in the way that best suits you.

This blank Team-Image Grid can be used to explore and analyze a team's success attributes. Add activities or attributes for the successful team that you envision.

			INDIVIDUAL STRATEGIC PLANNING							
			TEAM-IMAGE GRID							
	EXCELLENT		GOOD		FAIR			POOR		
TEAM-IMAGE	1	2	3	4	5	6	7	8	9	10
TEAM NAME (T):										
T1:										
T2:			COPYRIGHT- James S. Gordon 1994-2011							
T3:										

This graphic represents the first version of "The Goal Tree". You may display it in graphic form or in a narrative form - as you complete your individual strategic plan.

PERSONAL STRATEGIC PLANNING
w/ Goal Distillation Process

THE GOAL TREE

The Things That I Do

I Want/ Choose To Do   **I Have To Do**

Dream	Love	Like	Agree	Avoid	Must	Should	Agree
1._____	1._____	1._____	1._____	1._____	1._____	1._____	1._____
2._____	2._____	2._____	2._____	2._____	2._____	2._____	2._____
3._____	3._____	3._____	3._____	3._____	3._____	3._____	3._____

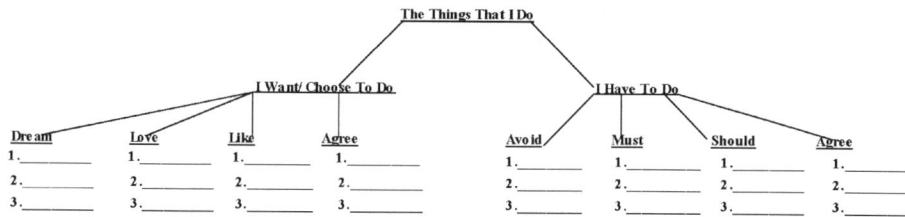

Questions regarding your "TO DO" activities:

1. Whose idea is this activity?

2. Why do it?

3. To be done by/ with whom?

4. How is it to be done?

5. What is to be done?

6. When is it to be done?

7. Where is it to be done?

8. If not done-what happens?

9. When done-what happens?

10. How do you feel about that?

11. Will you do it again?

12. Why or why not?

(Some) Goal Sources: Parents, Spouse, Children, Friends, Peers, Bosses, Co-workers, Church, Government, Other.

INSTRUCTIONS: On this page or another one, begin to list the things that you do in terms of "want tos" and "have tos".
Break down this list by the eight categories listed above, i.e. Dream, Love, Like, etc.

Although, this form has been re-done, the idea remains that you can list your needs and desires in terms of the priority that you assign to each - based on the output of The Goal Tree activity. This was the form used in numerous workshops

PERSONAL STRATEGIC PLANNING

w/ Goal Distillation Process

GOAL GRID

Intensity											Topics
W 10											Career
A 9											Community
N 8											Education
T 7											Family
6											Health
T 5											Marriage
O 4											Other
3											Personal
D 2											Social
O 1											Spiritual
	1	2	3	4	5	6	7	8	9	10	
	Lower—PRIORITY—Higher										
	H	A	V	E		T	O		D	O	

Instructions: List things that you would like to have/do under each goal "topic".

CAREER(CA)	COMMUNITY(CO)	EDUCATION(E)	FAMILY(F)	HEALTH(H)
1.	1.	1.	1.	1.
2.	2.	2.	2.	2.
3.	3.	3.	3.	3.
etc.	etc.	etc.	etc.	etc.

MARRIAGE(M)	PERSONAL(P)	SOCIAL(SO)	SPIRITUAL(SP)	OTHER(O)
1.	1.	1.	1.	1.
2.	2.	2.	2.	2.
3.	3.	3.	3.	3.
etc.	etc.	etc.	etc.	etc.

Place the abbreviation in parentheses ( ) inside the Goal Grid. For example, Family goal #1

Again, this is one of the first (linked) To Do Lists, which is completed after you completed The Goal Grid and The Goal Circles exercises.

PERSONAL STRATEGIC PLANNING
Goal Discovery & Distillation Process

TO DO LIST

1._____☐; U/P; Grid#____
2._____☐; U/P; Grid#____
3._____☐; U/P; Grid#____
4._____☐; U/P; Grid#____
5._____☐; U/P; Grid#____
6._____☐; U/P; Grid#____
7._____☐; U/P; Grid#____
8._____☐; U/P; Grid#____
9._____☐; U/P; Grid#____
10._____☐; U/P; Grid#____

TO DO LIST

1._____☐; U/P; Grid#____
2._____☐; U/P; Grid#____
3._____☐; U/P; Grid#____
4._____☐; U/P; Grid#____
5._____☐; U/P; Grid#____
6._____☐; U/P; Grid#____
7._____☐; U/P; Grid#____
8._____☐; U/P; Grid#____
9._____☐; U/P; Grid#____
10._____☐; U/P; Grid#____

TO DO LIST

1._____☐; U/P; Grid#____
2._____☐; U/P; Grid#____
3._____☐; U/P; Grid#____
4._____☐; U/P; Grid#____
5._____☐; U/P; Grid#____
6._____☐; U/P; Grid#____
7._____☐; U/P; Grid#____
8._____☐; U/P; Grid#____
9._____☐; U/P; Grid#____
10._____☐; U/P; Grid#____

TO DO LIST

1._____☐; U/P; Grid#____
2._____☐; U/P; Grid#____
3._____☐; U/P; Grid#____
4._____☐; U/P; Grid#____
5._____☐; U/P; Grid#____
6._____☐; U/P; Grid#____
7._____☐; U/P; Grid#____
8._____☐; U/P; Grid#____
9._____☐; U/P; Grid#____
10._____☐; U/P; Grid#____

TO DO LIST

1._____☐; U/P; Grid#____
2._____☐; U/P; Grid#____
3._____☐; U/P; Grid#____
4._____☐; U/P; Grid#____
5._____☐; U/P; Grid#____
6._____☐; U/P; Grid#____
7._____☐; U/P; Grid#____
8._____☐; U/P; Grid#____
9._____☐; U/P; Grid#____
10._____☐; U/P; Grid#____

TO DO LIST

1._____☐; U/P; Grid#____
2._____☐; U/P; Grid#____
3._____☐; U/P; Grid#____
4._____☐; U/P; Grid#____
5._____☐; U/P; Grid#____
6._____☐; U/P; Grid#____
7._____☐; U/P; Grid#____
8._____☐; U/P; Grid#____
9._____☐; U/P; Grid#____
10._____☐; U/P; Grid#____

Here is a look at The Success Model - used in early workshops. This arrangement shows a way to compare and contrast content among multiple individual or team models.

SUCCESSFUL ROLE MODEL(S):

A._____

B._____

C._____

WORDS:

1._____

2._____

3._____

4._____

5._____

DEEDS:

1._____

2._____

3._____

4._____

5._____

APPEARANCE:

1._____

2._____

3._____

4._____

5._____

SUCCESSFUL TEAM MODEL(S):

A._____

B._____

C._____

WORDS:

1._____

2._____

3._____

4._____

5._____

DEEDS:

1._____

2._____

3._____

4._____

5._____

APPEARANCE:

1._____

2._____

3._____

4._____

5._____

From my 3rd grade spelling bee to (hopefully) the publication of this ebook, we want to keep in mind successes and the feelings which go along with those envisioned successes.

PERSONAL STRATEGIC PLANNING
"DEJA VU"
Success Revisited

	ACCOMPLISHMENT(S):	EMOTION(S):
Last 12 mos.	(a)_____	_____
	(b)_____	_____
	(c)_____	_____
Last 5 years	(a)_____	_____
	(b)_____	_____
	(c)_____	_____
>10 yrs. ago	(a)_____	_____
	(b)_____	_____
	(c)_____	_____

	FUTURE ACCOMPLISHMENTS:	EMOTIONS:
Next 24 mos.	(a)_____	_____
	(b)_____	_____
	(c)_____	_____
Next 2-5 yrs.	(a)_____	_____
	(b)_____	_____
	(c)_____	_____

APPENDIX B

Goals Lexicon

1. GOAL: Goals are the components, which plans are first divided into.

2. GOAL-CENTERED: One who plans and achieves goals as a way of life.

3. GOAL ABANDONMENT: After one's goals are set one gives up on the realization of the goal - when/if adversity "befalls" her, him, or them.

4. GOAL ABSORPTION: To so involve oneself in a goal that the activity becomes even more than he or she "bargained" for...leading to the next logical (larger) goal(s).

5. GOAL ACCEPTANCE: To agree to attain a goal generated by someone else or perhaps a team.

6. GOAL ACQUIESCENCE: The initial reluctance and resistance to the pursuit of a goal, which gives way to the accomplishment.

7. GOAL ADDICTION: An unhealthy fixation on the setting of goals or any single component of the Vision Continuum, i.e. Visions, Missions, Plans, Goals, Objectives, or Tasks.

8. GOAL ADHESION : Goals which stick with us/in our minds even when we do not pursue the goal, e.g. through writing the goal, and developing action plans, etc. (the someday goal).

9. GOAL ADULTERATION: Mixing of goals and objectives or vision and mission; also mixing of goal setting systems and components of the Vision Continuum.

10. GOAL ADVOCACY: Initiating a pro goal-setting posture for the benefit of others.

11. GOAL AFTERGLOW: The sense of euphoria, gratitude or satisfaction that comes from goal attainment / alignment.

12. GOAL ALIENATION: To allow oneself to become so estranged to one's goals or goals "forced upon" you that you want nothing to do with the goal or goal-setting, in general.

13. GOAL AMALGAMS: Activities, which overlap into several goal areas-thus "getting two birds with one stone".

14. GOAL ANTECENDENTS: Visions, missions and plans.

15. GOAL ASSESSMENT: The Goal Discovery and Distillation Process...(GDDP).

16. GOAL ASSAY: Done via The Goal Gauge - the tool which helps to quantify the intensity of needs and wants.

17. GOAL AUTOPSY: A review or audit to determine why a goal was not attained.

18. GOAL BACKFIRE: When one sets an incomplete goal as discussed in "The Goal Discovery and Distillation Process" one can get the opposite or other unintended result.

19. GOAL BALANCE: When goals are set and pursued in each [most] of the areas of the Goal Grid.

20. GOAL BALKING: The false starts which causes the starting and stopping of the pursuit of a goal or goals.

21. GOAL BARGAINING: The process of obtaining the resources, priority and/or commitment to pursue a goal(s), typically with another individual or others.

22. GOAL BARRICADES: Perceived road blocks to the accomplishment of a goal selected by others/another.

23. GOAL BARTER: Exchanging goals, resources, commitments, permissions or other requisites for goal attainment.

24. GOAL BEREAVEMENT: The sense of loss when a goal is abandoned or precluded by forces beyond one's control.

25. GOAL BIAS: The belief that goal-setting doesn't work...for me or that it's for others preferring another means of attaining.

26. GOAL BLEND: Is the deliberate attempt to collaborate on the achievement of a goal---as in a family or work team.

27. GOAL BLUFF: Gamesmanship regarding goals proclamation pertaining to goal accomplishment, resources and/or commitments not based on facts.

28. GOAL BREAKDOWN STRUCTURE: Vision Continuum - goals progeny, action plan.

29. GOAL BROADCASTING: Putting others on notice-verbally or in writing that you are going to do / obtain / attain a thing.

30. GOAL BUFFERS: Excuses, rationale for not pursuing or attaining a goal(s).

31. GOAL BY-PRODUCTS: Getting results other than those planned --both positive and negative results.

32. GOAL CEILING: The point of highest expectations regarding goals to pursue and what can be attained by a given individual, team or group.

33. GOAL CELEBRATION: Celebrating the process of goal – getting as well as the desired outcome before it is realized.

34. GOAL CHEAT(ING): Taking unethical or illegal shortcuts to a goal; or lying about its accomplishment.

35. GOAL CIRCLES: A tool to compare and contrast goals between two or more parties. A GDDP form.

36. GOAL CLARIFICATION: The process of attaining clear direction as to the desired outcomes - using the GDDP.

37. GOAL CLARITY: What should happen after completing this workbook, i.e. "How to Succeed at Personal Planning and Goal Setting.

38. GOAL CLOUDING: Allowing Pseudo-goals to mix with goals gained via the GDDP. OR when "Want Tos" become "Have Tos".

39. GOAL CLUSTERS: Closely-related goals within a "category" of goals, e.g. Family, Career, Health, etc.---which may lead to a "domino" effect in terms of accomplishing the goals.

40. GOAL CLUTTER: Remnants of prior goal-setting and planning efforts - occurs when one does not purge goals on a periodic basis.

41. GOAL COALESCENCE: Planned or unplanned goal synergy.

42. GOAL COASTING: Resting on one's laurels after a major goal is accomplished.

43. GOAL COLLABORATION: Enlisting the "aid" of another (others) in the accomplishment of a goal.

44. GOAL COMITY: Peaceful recognition and co-existence of goals among family, team or co-workers.

45. GOAL COMPETITION: When equal priority is assigned to goals in the Goal Grid-there will likely be competition for your time. And work goals can "encroach" on family goals as with the Goal Circle exercise.

46. GOAL COMPONENTS: Refer to both the components of the GDDP and the steps taken to complete it.

47. GOAL COMPOSITE: Result of goal negotiation or goal compromise - an outcome that incorporates input from multiple individuals.

48. GOAL COMPROMISE: Process of relinquishing some of the desired outcomes of one's goal(s) or the give-and-take of coming to an agreement on the other aspects of the Vision Continuum [Vision Mapping process].

49. GOAL CONCEPTION: Takes place when one is developing goals for the Goal Grid; and they occur spontaneously---then are written down for immediate or later use.

50. GOAL CONFLICT: Occurs when two or more opposing goals OR a "have to / need to" and a "want to / choose to" collide.

51. GOAL CONFUSION: Comes when someone else asks for your help and the outcome has not been sufficiently conveyed to you or when you simply are not sure what to do or how to proceed in pursuit of a goal.

52. GOAL CONSCRIPTION: Comes from someone else and is forced on you by circumstances beyond your control.

53. GOAL CONSTRICTION: Factors outside one's control, which lead to the alteration of one's goal(s) so that he or she gets/does less than was planned.

54. GOAL CONVERGENCE: Finding oneself at a point where achieving one's goal leads to or partially/wholly satisfies another goal. Or two or more people may find "common ground"...

55. GOAL COUNTERFEITS: Psuedo-goals, incomplete goals. Not specific or measurable.

56. GOAL COWARDS: A goal coward might say, "Goal-setting didn't work for me then and I

ain't gonna waste my time doing it again!"

57. GOAL CREATION: The outcome of using the GDDP.

58. GOAL CREDIBILITY(IN): The belief that you can achieve your goals or the belief you can't.

59. GOAL CREEP: What starts out to be Goal A ends up being Goal B or Goal C.

60. GOAL CRYSTALLIZATION: Happens when a goal remains long after your belief in your ability to make it happen is gone.

61. GOAL CUSTOMIZING: Refers to fine tuning goals through the GDDP Feedback System.

62. GOAL CYCLING: Going from goal to the next, without completing the previous goal

63. GOAL DECLINATION: Refers to the "erosion" in the magnitude/scope of the goal.

64. GOAL DEFINITION: : Goal Breakdown Structure yields goal definition and refinement.

65. GOAL DEFLATION: This usually happens when people try to talk you out of the goal-so as to not see/have you disappointed. And sometimes we do it to ourselves.

66. GOAL DEJA VU: The concept that a user can recall previously attained goals and the attendant emotions to re-create the energy needed to bring the new goal to pass. A GDDP Form

67. GOAL DELETION: Process of updating goals (desire and priority) dropping goals that were no longer desired or needed.

68. GOAL DENIAL: Stating that one has no goals or believes goal-setting is ineffective.

69. GOAL DEPENDENCE: Belief that someone or something else must happen before one's goal can be achieved.

70. GOAL DIFFUSION: When we bite off more than we can chew, our energies are typically diffused over these multiple projects.

71. GOAL DILUTION: Adding on activities not related which "sap" one of his or her energy.

72. GOAL DIMINUTION: Accepting less and less of an original goal.

73. GOAL DISCRIMINATION: The process of deciding on activities that are goal-related excluding those which are not.

74. GOALS DISCUSSION GROUPS: Online chat fora for goals.

75. GOAL DISDAIN: Looking down on goal-setting and goal-getters with loathing or contempt.

76. GOAL DISILLUSIONMENT: Becoming unhappy with the lack of progress one makes or isn't making towards achieving one's goals.

77. GOAL DISINTEGRATION: Allowing one's plan to fall apart for lack of attention or desire for the end product/outcome.

78. GOAL DISSONANCE: Holding/writing a goal and its anti-goal or counter-goal in mind at the same time.

79. GOAL DISTANCING: Placing the specifics of a goal so far in the future; or making it so complex that realization of the goal becomes remote.

80. GOAL DISTILLATION PROCESS: The forms and processes that are part of the Individual Strategic Planning process.

81. GOAL DISTRIBUTION: Doling or meting out of goals by a leader, manager, head of household or person in charge of a group activity.

82. GOAL DIVERGENCE: Recognizing that a goal is separate and distinct from a goal it was "mated" with or paired with.

83. GOAL DORMANCY: "Remembering" a goal from long ago-which still is a strong "want to".

84. GOAL DUMPING: Relegating to someone else our goal activities.

85. GOAL EMIGRATION: "Buying" into someone else's goals (want tos)-making it our own or joint in nature.

86. GOAL ENLARGEMENT: Simply adding on to a goal (quantity not quality).

87. GOAL ENRICHMENT: Adding on to a goal (qualitatively).

88. GOAL ENVY: Coveting the actual goal of another or another's goal-setting prowess.

89. GOAL EXCITEMENT: Enthusiasm, Expectation/Belief in a goal's achievement. The joy, thrill, and/or excitement that comes from the pursuit of worthwhile goals.

90. GOAL EXCLUSIVITY: "Clearing the calendar" to do a goal.

91. GOAL EXUBERANCE: The state of unabated joy, ecstasy regarding the expectation and imminent realization of a goal(s).

92. GOAL FAILURE: A goal that is not realized because one gives up on it or abandons it.

93. GOAL FANATIC: One who becomes overbearing regarding the imposition of her or his zeal for goal-setting.

94. GOAL FAST: A planned time wherein one does not consciously pursue her or his goals.

95. GOAL FATIGUE: The belief that goals tire one out or take too much energy to accomplish.

96. GOAL FEVER: Typically happens when a goal is accomplished and one immediately wants to pursue one or more goals right away with great passion.

97. GOAL FISHING: Trying on/brainstorming "suitable' goals for oneself.

98. GOAL FIT: Finding the right goal and becoming excited about it.

99. GOAL FLOOR: The point where one does not want to go below in terms of the expectations of goal quality, goal quantity.

100. GOAL FORECASTING: Using the Critical Success Factors of the Goal Gauge to predict the successful attainment of a goal(s) or the possible failure...

101. GOAL FORENSICS: Using the Critical Success Factors of the Goal Gauge to determine why a goal failed to be achieved or was achieved.

102. GOAL FRACTURING: Happens when goals are re-apportioned due to non-accomplishment, conflict, etc.

103. GOAL FUNK: A point of pause wherein goal doubt or uncertainty prevail.

104. GOAL FUSION: Purposeful melding of goals.

105. GOAL GAP: Can be seen when The Vision Continuum is missing one or more components.

106. GOAL GAUGE: Forensics and forecasting tool used in the GDDP.

107. GOAL GENESIS: The Goal Tree - when, where and why.

108. GOAL GESTALT: Rehearsing and Celebrating an outcome--buying a TV cart prior to buying the TV.

109. GOAL GESTATION: The period that one thinks about/dreams about the outcome before the goal is realized.

110. GOAL GETTER: One who sets and attains goals.

111. GOAL GLOAT: The person or process of bragging about one's goal attainment or quantity or quantity of goals.

112. GOAL GLORIFICATION: Believing goal-setting is somehow magical and that it can change lives; and that anybody can/should "naturally" do it/know how to do it.

113. GOAL GOLD: The right combination/selection of goals that inspire an emotional and psychic commitment to one's goals.

114. GOAL GRAPHICS: A non-narrative, written/pictorial presentation of goals.

115. GOAL GRID: One of the tools in the GDDP.

116. GOAL GRIDLOCK: Happens when priorities are not set and each "goal", i.e. have tos and want tos "clamor" for your attention.

117. GOAL HARMONY: Intra-goal and/or inter-goal congruence.

118. GOAL HATRED: One who is so disenchanted with what they believe to be goal-setting that they won't listen to an explanation of what it really is because of the "bad taste" in their mouth.

119. GOAL HERESY: Bad-mouthing the inputs, processes and outputs of planning and goal-setting.

120. GOAL HIATUS: Planned or unplanned pull-back from the pursuit of one or more goals.

121. GOAL HIERARCHIES: Sequenced/staggered goals; often times "compressed" to a point where steps are missing/ not well-defined.

122. GOAL HOARDING: I can do mine and yours and their goals; assuming goals which may interfere with the accomplishment of your own goals.

123. GOAL HOSTILITY: Animus towards the outcome or process of goal-setting and the people who engage in the same.

124. GOAL HUMOR: Anecdotes and jokes about goals and goal-setting.

125. GOAL HYBRIDS : See Goal Blends, Amalgams---intra-goal and inter-goal combinations.

126. GOAL HYPE: This is the best thing since sliced bread "spiel"- achievers tell everyone who'll listen.

127. GOAL HYPERBOLE: An exaggerated goal or exaggerated accounting of goal accomplishment.

128. GOAL HYPOCRITES: Those who champion goal-setting, but don't take time to write or evaluate their own goals.

129. GOAL IDENTIFICATION: Takes place during the GDDP.

130. GOAL IMITATION: Eschewing the GDDP by copying or borrowing from others' goals.

131. GOAL IMMERSION: Learning and living the goal discovery and distillation process and becoming conversant in the goal lexicon.

132. GOAL IMMIGRATION: Takes place when/as others "buy in" to your goals.

133. GOAL IMPERIALISM: I know what's best for you-do it my way or else.

134. GOAL IMPOSTORS: Unwritten wishes and hopes/fantasies.

135. GOAL INCOMPATIBILITY: Goals, if realized will give you a different or opposite result from the one you intended...more specifically these are activities/objectives (components of goals).

136. GOAL INDEPENDENCE: Goals that are "segregated" so as to do one at a time.

137. GOAL INERTIA: The feeling of enormity emanating from the thought of pursuing a goal(s) - typically caused by the lack of a Goal Breakdown Structure, which "sizes" the goal into manageable "chunks" of actions.

138. GOAL INFATUATION: A feeling of well-being coming from another's goals or another's attainment of a goal(s).

139. GOAL INFIDELITY: Foregoing one's own goals in favor of another's, giving one's best to others' goals while neglecting one's personal goals.

140. GOAL INFLATION: Talking up (puffing) a goal so as to make oneself look important.

141. GOAL INHERITANCE: Typically takes place when you assume/must assume activities that were previously done by someone else who no longer can/will do it.

142. GOAL INPUT: Goal Tree, Goal Grid, and Goal Circles.

143. GOAL INTEGRATION: Developing mutual goals.

144. GOAL INTERDEPENDENCE: Recognizing how goals interrelate.

145. GOAL INTOLERANCE: Refusing any attempt to have someone help you with goal-setting. Rejecting others' goals.

146. GOAL INVASION: An attempt(s) to have you take on someone else's goals by cajoling/coercion.

147. GOAL ISOLATION: Dropping everything one is doing to concentrate on a goal or doing everything else-but "the goal".

148. GOAL JEALOUSY: Happens when another chooses to pursue her / his own goal and your adverse reaction to that choice(s).

149. GOAL JUSTIFICATION: Developing the rationale for a goal choice(s).

150. GOAL LINKING: Choosing activities that "cross-over" between goals.

151. GOAL LUST: A strong attraction and attachment to another's goal(s).

152. GOAL MALINGERING: Procrastinating, stewing in the process or after the accomplishment of a goal.

153. GOAL MEASUREMENT: Determining the degree to which a goal is (being) accomplished.

154. GOAL MEDIATION: A process that mitigates the goal conflict brought on by the Goal Circles, exercises.

155. GOAL MESSAGE BOARD: Online, moderated discussion group.

156. GOAL METRICS: Critical Success Factors---from the Goal Gauge [and CFFs]

157. GOAL MINING: Process of discovering goals used in the GDDP.

158. GOAL MIS-MATCH: Taking on a goal that disagrees with you due to your temperament or training.

159. GOAL MODEL: A diagram or graphic representation of a goal; an example of a goal based on the Vision Continuum.

160. GOAL MONITORING: The oversight, review and evaluation of goals.

161. GOAL MORPHING: The conscious manipulation of a goal to change it into another goal.

162. GOAL MOURNING: The sadness which comes from the cessation of the pursuit of one's goal(s)...goal failure's aftermath.

163. GOAL MYOPIA: Not seeing short-term doable activities to further your goals.

164. GOAL NEOPHYTE: One who is just getting started with the GDDP.

165. GOAL NESTING: The unfolding of one goal within another goal - 2 or more levels deep.

166. GOAL NULLIFICATION: Giving up and starting all over. Being fired from a job can cause some goal nullification.

167. GOAL OBSESSION: Typically comes when a person needs to feel a sense of accomplishing and therefore sets an endless string of goals or gets inextricably tied into the process...

168. GOAL ONE-UPMANSHIP: Purposefully enlarging/enriching a goal to outdo another.

169. GOAL ORIENTATION ANALYSIS : A step in the GDDP [Goal Circles].

170. GOAL ORPHAN: A worthwhile project that goes "begging" because someone hasn't/doesn't do the initial "grunt work" to make it happen.

171. GOAL OSCILLATION: Meandering back and forth between goals---a little here and a little there.

172. GOAL OUTCOME: End result or desired outcome.

173. GOAL OVERHAUL: Going back to the "drawing board" to redo goals that are "problematic".

174. GOAL OVERLAP: The intentional/unintentional development of goals that are similar/very similar so as to be done simultaneously/consecutively.

175. GOAL OVERLOAD: Happens when we've added on to the goal or simply become impatient and try to do too much/too soon.

176. GOAL OWNERSHIP: Comes from either developing the goals ourselves or from assuming goals from another source.

177. GOAL PARALYSIS: Happens when the details of the process get the better of you or perhaps its fear of failing to accomplish the goal causing "immobility".

178. GOAL PARITY: Perceived equality of goals between people, teams or institutions.

179. GOAL PASSION: The strong, persistent desire to be engaged in goal-setting and goal-getting.

180. GOAL PAUPER: One without a goal-setting system and/or a few disorganized goals.

181. GOAL PHOBIA: Unrealistic fear of the practice or outcome of goal-setting.

182. GOAL PLAGIARISM: When someone takes a piece of the goal without our knowledge, or we take from others goals and claim that they are ours/we did it.

183. GOAL PLATEAUING: Happens when a goal is accomplished and no new goal is established.

184. GOAL POLARIZATION: When in the process of defining goals and developing action plans, we find a goal/activity that stands out because it is so unlike other goals/activities.

185. GOAL POSTPONEMENT: Putting off the date/time of realizing a goal.

186. GOAL POST-MORTEM: A review or audit to determine why a goal was or was not attained.

187. GOAL POSTURE: A snapshot of our current goals.

188. GOAL POVERTY: Lack of goals and/or goal setting system by a group, team or organization.

189. GOAL PROSPECTING: Using another (non-GDP) system to find/discover one's goals.

190. GOAL PRIORITIZATION: Takes place during the Goal Grid portion of the GDP.

191. GOAL PROGENY: Objectives, Tasks or "To Do" items and action plans.

192. GOAL PROMISCUITY: Becoming so eclectic that we jump on any "high sounding" goal without much thought.

193. GOAL PRUNING: Getting rid of activities that are not beneficial to the accomplishment of our goals.

194. GOAL PUFFING: The "white lies" one tells to embellish their goals, goal-setting or goal-getting prowess.

195. GOAL REALIZATION: Accomplishment of the goal.

196. GOAL RECIPROCITY: Activities which help two or more people achieve mutual goals.

197. GOAL RECONCILIATION: Overcoming goal conflict through collaboration or evaluation of competing goals.

198. GOAL REDUNDANCY: Two or more activities that will accomplish the same/similar goals.

199. GOAL REFOCUS: When we are sidetracked from our goals or new want tos/have tos come into being, we then refocus/re-assess our priorities...

200. GOAL RENEWAL: Dusting off goals that have become dormant/stale/sidetracked.

201. GOAL RESISTANCE: A holding back from "commitment" to a goal(s).

202. GOAL RETREAT: Typically happens when a goal has been "assumed" from another/by another; and interest has since waned.

203. GOAL REVELATION: "Ahas" from engagement with the process, i.e. GDDP.

204. GOAL REVIVAL: Re-committing and/or re-focusing on goals that have been "set aside".

205. GOAL ROLL-BACK: Determining the plan, which gave rise to the goal. Then determining the mission, which gave rise to the plan. And, finally determining the mission, which gave rise to the vision - one step at a time.

206. GOAL SABOTAGE: Activities designed to prevent the accomplishment of another's goals; occasionally one sabotages one's own goals.

207. GOAL SCAPEGOATING: Blaming individuals or groups for one's lack of success, resources or system for goal-getting.

208. GOAL SCENARIO: Envisioning a desired outcome and what it would be like to have, to be, or to share the goal.

209. GOAL SCHOLAR: One who studies goals---keeps track of any/all innovations in this field---sometimes to her detriment in terms of her own personal goal-setting.

210. GOAL SEGREGATION: See Goal Isolation.

211. GOAL SHY: Tacit about goals, secretive.

212. GOAL SIZING: Changing one's goals to match one's energy/belief/mood.

213. GOAL SNOB: One who believes themselves superior because they write and study goal-setting---and thinks themselves better than those who don't.

214. GOAL SPIN-OFF: An activity you find that you enjoy/want to do as a result of the goal-setting process (a new activity).

215. GOAL STACKING: Adding on more and different activities usually to the detriment of the initial goals.

216. GOAL STAGGERING: A technique used to accomplish goals in a sequential/ logical/ efficient manner.

217. GOAL STIGMA: Perceived ill-feelings (thoughts) regarding one's potential non-success regarding a goal failure.

218. GOAL SUBORDINATION: Used in tandem with Goal Staggering allows for greater likelihood of success.

219. GOAL SUBSTITUTION: Choosing an alternate goal that one perceives to be more or equally efficacious to the current or former goal.

220. GOAL SUN-BURNING: Becoming so enthusiastic about your goal-setting prowess/success that we "insist" that others do likewise - whether they want to or not (this is an unintentionally overbearing individual).

221. GOAL SURGE: The energy that comes from the momentum one gains while pursuing a goal(s) and/or the rush of new goals or new ideas regarding goal attainment.

222. GOAL SWAPPING: Bartering - quid pro quos.

223. GOAL SYNERGY: The energy that comes from the momentum built by combining cognitive and affective and behavioral efforts towards agreed upon goals and plans.

224. GOAL SYNONYMS: Objectives, end results, outcomes, milestones, aims, purposes, missions - from major reference books.

225. GOAL SYNTHESIS: Taking two or more goals and recombining them into one or more new goals/activities.

226. GOAL TABOO: Outcome or object of goal is considered socially or politically inappropriate.

227. GOAL TEAMING: Enlisting the aid of another/others to attain a goal.

228. GOAL TEASING: One who has completed a goal or series of goals that "eggs on" another/others.

229. GOAL TIME-OUT: Scheduled time away from the pursuit of a goal - even to work on another goal or others' goals.

230. GOAL TIMIDITY: Reservation or fear of setting or pursuing a goal(s).

231. GOAL TINKERING: Usually engaging in make-work activities rather than actual objectives of the goal.

232. GOAL TRADE-OFFS: Taking progress on one or more goals at the expense of other goals.

233. GOAL TRANSITION: The movement from an accomplished goal to a new goal.

234. GOAL TRAUMA: The upset due to setbacks in this process or the upset attendant to obtaining the wrong end result.

235. GOAL TREE: A GDDP form

236. GOAL TRESPASS: Invading/interrupting the process of another's goal getting or likewise having another invade your goal getting...

237. GOAL TRIAL: A toe in the water approach to goal-setting - a test drive

238. GOAL TROLL: A naysayer who always has a negative prediction or thought/word about another's goal-setting success or prospects for success.

239. GOAL TYRANT: One who "thrusts" goals on subordinates, children or others who she or he directs.

240. GOAL VACILLATION: On again off again relationship with goals/goal setting. Now you see them - now you don't.

241. GOAL VISTA: A vantage point wherein one can see the whole picture in regards to her or his goal.

242. GOAL WIPE-OUT": Abandonment of goals due to failure or fear of failure.

243. GOAL WRITING: Reducing our goals to writing.

244. GOAL YEARNING: Typically, the desire that precedes the writing of one's goals.

245. GOALSPEAK: The nomenclature, lexicon, dialect or language of goal setting and planning. What occurs as we incorporate the foregoing lexicon or glossary into our every-day conversation or language.

Book Jacket

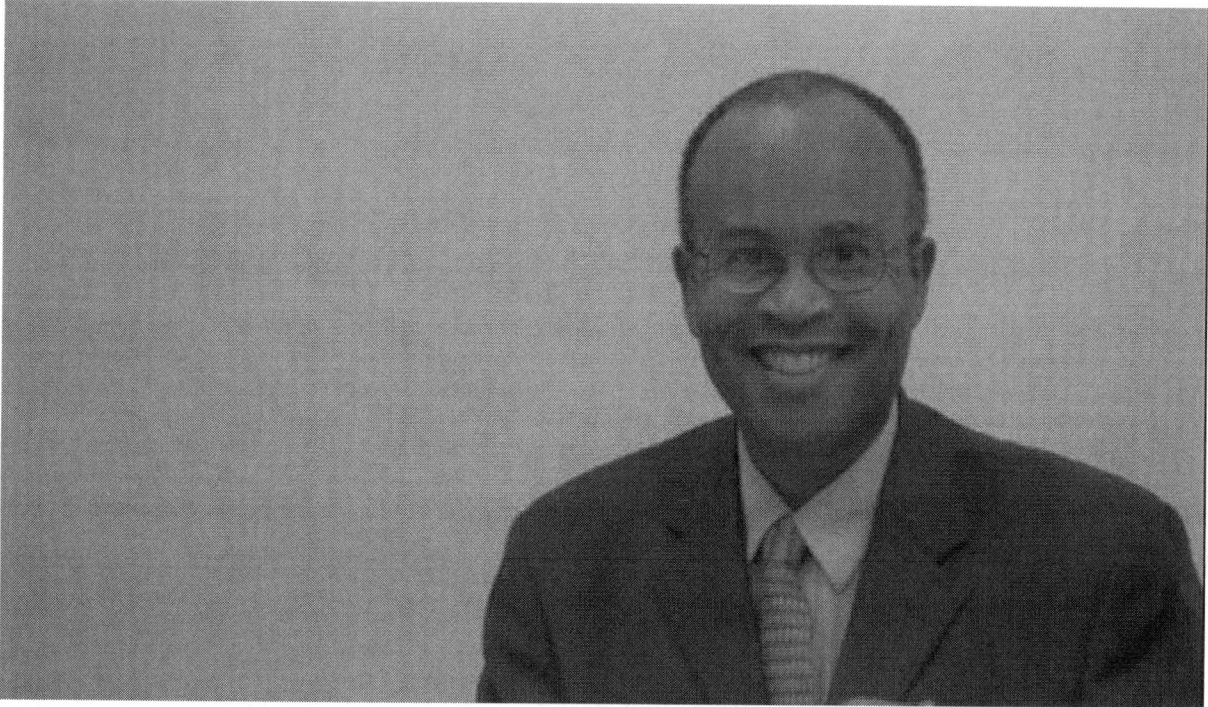

About the Author

Jim has extensive experience training adults in the areas of human resource development, workforce development, and entrepreneur success training.

His experience as a business owner has included consulting in the areas of financial services, life skills training, and job search. He has also run an online business, which sold health and nutrition products, internationally.

Jim has earned a Bachelors of Science - Secondary Education, a Masters of Business Administration - with an emphasis in Project Management, and at this writing, he has completed all the requirements for his doctorate in Applied Management and Decision Sciences, except his dissertation.

Jim resides in southeastern Washington State with his wife, Bonnie. They have three adult children, Jamila, Jay, and Jonathan.

Made in the USA
Lexington, KY
06 August 2019